There is a Message of Hope for Today in our Life Mess

THE Mess HAS THE Message

OVERCOME DEPRESSION AND ANXIETY WITH
12 SPIRITUAL AFFIRMATIONS
TO EMBRACE LIFE CHANGES

GRATITUDE JOURNAL INCLUDED

R.K. CHOGA

COPYRIGHT

The events and conversations in this book have been set down to the best of the author's ability, although some names and details have been left out to protect the privacy of individuals. Copyright © 2023 by EZY AZ ABC All rights reserved. No part of this book may be reproduced or used in any manner without written permission of the copyright owner except for the use of quotations in a book review. For more information, Website: www.ezyazabc.com.

Scripture quotations marked (AMP) are taken from the Amplified® Bible (AMP), Copyright © 2015 by The Lockman Foundation. Used by permission. lockman.org.

Scripture quotations marked (ESV) are from The ESV® Bible (The Holy Bible, English Standard Version®), © 2001 by Crossway, a publishing ministry of Good News Publishers. Used by permission. All rights reserved.

Scripture quotations marked (GNT) are from the Good News Translation in Today's English Version – Second Edition Copyright © 1992 by American Bible Society. Used by Permission.

Scripture quotations marked (KJV) are from The Authorized (King James) Version. Rights in the Authorized Version in the United Kingdom are vested in the Crown. Reproduced by permission of the Crown's patentee, Cambridge University Press.

Scripture quotations marked (MSG) are from The Message. Copyright © 1993, 1994, 1995, 1996, 2000, 2001, 2002. Used by permission of NavPress Publishing Group.

Scripture quotations marked (NIV) are taken from the Holy Bible, New International Version®, NIV®. Copyright © 1973, 1978, 1984, 2011 by Biblica, Inc.™ Used by permission of Zondervan. All rights reserved worldwide. www.zondervan.com. The "NIV" and "New International Version" are trademarks registered in the United States Patent and Trademark Office by Biblica, Inc.™

Scripture quotations marked (NKJV) are taken from the New King James Version®. Copyright © 1982 by Thomas Nelson. Used by permission. All rights reserved.

Scripture quotations marked (NLT) are taken from the *Holy Bible*, New Living Translation, copyright ©1996, 2004, 2015 by Tyndale House Foundation. Used by permission of Tyndale House Publishers, Carol Stream, Illinois 60188. All rights reserved.

DISCLAIMER

The author makes no guarantees that your life will be transformed in the way hers has been. The book is based on her experience. You should seek the relevant professional assistance to help you with your journey.

This book is not intended to be a substitute for professional medical advice, diagnosis or treatment. Always seek the advice of your physician or other qualified health provider with any questions you may have regarding a medical condition.

At the time of writing or publishing, the author is not affiliated with and does not endorse anyone or any of the corporate entities mentioned in or involved in the distribution of this work, or any third-party entities whose trademarks and logos may appear in this work.

In the book of Psalms, David writes:

> "For you formed my inward parts; you knitted me together in my mother's womb. I praise you, for I am fearfully and wonderfully made. Wonderful are your works; my soul knows it very well." (Psalms 139:13-14 English Standard Version (ESV))

> *Fearfully* when translated from Hebrew means with great reverence, heart-felt interest and with respect. *Wonderfully* when translated from Hebrew means *unique and set apart.*[1]

ACKNOWLEDGEMENTS

The Mess Has The Message started off with 700+ pages of my different journals from 2017, the year my daughter was born, to 2022, when she started her first year of primary school (prep). It was quite a tome, and I didn't know where to start shaping it into something meaningful and helpful. I also struggled with the delivery of the message of hope in a positive manner whilst considering all the relationships involved as it was birthed from the mess in my life.

Each journal had a message when I wrote it, but when I first put it all together, it seemed like a total mess. Interestingly, I had already titled the book *The Mess Has The Message*. This was based on how my life was a mess, but at each turn, I saw a message of hope.

I struggled for an entire year from 2020 when I put it all together and failed to extract that 'message' from what now seemed like a literal 'mess' of pages until the end of 2021, when it all came together beautifully like a symphony.

I find myself wanting to individually thank everyone who has touched my life as they have played a part in this message, but I must summarise – not my strongest suit, considering how this book started!

This might seem typical, but it is most sincere and from the bottom of my heart to thank everyone. Thank you to my family, friends, friends who became family, neighbours, therapists, colleagues, my work family, the people I have come across in my day-to-day interactions, my church family, sisterhood and above all – God almighty, three in one – the Father, Son and Holy Spirit – my personal counsellor and peace. This book would truly not be possible without any of you. Thank you!

To my daughter, I am thankful and honoured by you, my girl, making me a mother. Yes, I love you just the way you are – you are the best, excellent, the lioness and heart of God, very holy.

CONTENTS

Introduction 1

Listen 5

Believe & Faith 9

PART 1 – Through the Struggles, Challenges, Hurt and Pain

Humble 17

Peace 29

PART 2 – Through the Walk

Confidence & Patience 45

Courage 69

PART 3 – Through the Recovery, Self-Discovery, Battles and Victory to the End

Forgive 89

Love 111

Thanks & Praise 129

PART 4 – Seasons

Winter Is Just a Season 183

Conclusion 215

About The Author 225

Reviews 227

Freebies 229

References 231

INTRODUCTION

Finding the Message in Your Mess

> The Mess = The Message

In the process of baking something beautiful, the kitchen counter is messy with broken eggshells, flour, milk, dough, you name it. At that stage, all you can see is a giant mess, but you know at the end, there will be some beautiful smelling baked goodies, like bread or whatever it is you like. The mixture will go in the oven for the heat to work on it and form a final product. It is like that with the mess in our life. We must go through what seems like a fiery furnace, an oven, to produce a better version of ourselves. In those messy stages we tend not to appreciate the process as we would if it were an actual baking process. For us to get the lovely loaf of fresh bread or baked goodies and the accompanying aroma, we must embrace the mess that comes with baking. We've got to learn how to do that with our life struggles to get to the improved version of ourselves.

This story entails what I learned from my baking process and the baked goodies I got from it with the hope of helping you with your process. It has my spiritual walk with God rooted in it, for that was my turning point from dark, murky waters.

The aim is for the book to be relatable regardless of your background or stage in life. Besides song snippets, I have also included references to movies, stories or other forms of inspiration that I discovered on my journey in the hope others can relate to them to get even a morsel of the message of hope on how to battle depression, anxiety and life's challenges, despite our differences.

From my baking process – the mess in my life – I got the message that I will detail in the chapters to come as the following twelve affirmations – **listen**, **believe**, have **faith**, be **humble** and at **peace**, have **confidence**, **patience** and **courage**, **forgive**, **love**, and above all, give **thanks** and **praise**. They are each based on a revelation of God's miracle or mighty deed that now stands as a memorial from which to draw strength and use in my life. Giving **thanks** and **praise** is the foundation of these affirmations.

I say it's how you choose to deal with life's mess that defines who you are: Do you get bogged down in the mess, or do you find the message of hope and work on that?

In the book of Psalms 77, the writer, during challenging times, says,

> "11 I will remember the deeds of the Lord;
>
> yes, I will remember your miracles of long ago.
>
> 12 I will consider all your works,
>
> and meditate on all your mighty deeds." (Psalms 77:11-12 New International Version (NIV))

(Note: The scripture passages in this book are from various versions of the Bible; this is in keeping with its collage style.)

Who I Am

My name is Ruvimbo Kudzai Choga.

Ruvimbo means hope, believe, faith and trust.

Kudzai means respect, praise, glory and honour.

INTRODUCTION

I was brought up in a Christian home, and so the full meaning behind my name with this in mind is:

– hope, believe; faith; trust in the Lord – praise, respect, give glory and honour the Lord.

My daughter's name is Tinotenda Arianah.

I am:

Amai Tinotenda – Tinotenda's mother: 'We thank you; we give thanks; we are thankful, grateful' that is the Shona (language of Zimbabwe) meaning that first comes to mind, although it is an ambiguous name with a deeper meaning, which I only discovered later down the track after a great deal of soul searching during my struggles.

Months after giving birth, I felt really lost in life – in my marriage, as a person, wife and new mother, not knowing who I was. I sought to understand and rediscover myself, plus accept who and where I was. I realised that Tinotenda is truly like a reiteration of Ruvimbo or who I am, the values that were to be instilled in not only our daughter, but myself, too, as it also means 'We have hope, believe, trust, faith'.

At that point in my life, it felt like my attention was being called to my name, to use it as a starting point, to see that this is who I am and never forget it. I needed to remember that Tinotenda means an 'attitude of gratitude' and 'giving thanks' and use it to fight my battles.

Amai Arianah – Arianah's mother – very holy (Greek), the best/excellent; Ari – the Lioness and Heart of God (Hebrew). This led me to the lioness arising within me to get out of my head and wake up to change my world.

Although I was brought up in a Christian home, my journey to fully understanding that my spirituality was not about my being forced to go to church and all the rest when I was younger came full circle only as an adult, with some ups and downs along the way. I realised that just as we feed ourselves and exercise for our physical and mental health – for our body, we have to do the same for our spiritual health, too – for our soul. Having a personal relationship with God and reflecting on that in my day-to-day life is of utter importance to me. This realisation and understanding only sank in deepest when my life was a complete mess – I was going through a painful separation and divorce, trying to sell a seemingly unsellable house, and suffering anxiety and depression as a consequence.

I am still learning, although what I know and believe in with absolute certainty is that even if I had a different name, my truest identity is that I am a child of God, and I am who he says I am: 'fearfully and wonderfully made'. I am unique and set apart with a story of my own to share with the world.

The spiritual affirmations in this book are from a story I have puzzled and collaged together using my journals, memories, encounters, testimonies, songs, movies and experiences of a life that has been tortuous, broken, chaotic, steep, difficult, yet rewarding, full and ultimately very surprising: with the messes in my life turning into a message of hope and joy.

To form a habit, we need to consistently put it into practice over a certain period until it comes naturally to us. Feel free to pick an affirmation to actively follow through daily for a set period. You can start with the first one in this book – **listen**. Meditate on it, journal, collage, or follow through in whatever way appeals to you or your creativity to keep track of what you get from applying and being alert to that affirmation throughout that time frame.

LISTEN

> LISTEN – be **quick to listen** and slow to talk.
>
> *(the message in James 1:19)*

As I struggled to listen to a certain speaker because I perceived them as arrogant, it reminded me of an analogy that someone once shared. If I had a diamond covered in dirt to give you, would you find it valuable? If it was covered in poo, would you still find it of similar value? It was a rhetorical question posed to several people and in my heart of hearts, I was sure, like so many others, that unequivocally the answer was a yes and yes. If I apply this analogy to the speaker who I was having trouble listening to, I shouldn't have allowed my perception of them to negate the value in their message.

> "I want every person I encounter to know they have value. When you know your value, you begin to live valued."
>
> *Bronwen Healy (author and speaker)*

I believe whatever we go through, if we take the time to **listen** and not have our mouths and minds run wild with our noisy talk and thoughts, we will find value and the answer we need. This is something I have learned and keep relearning every day to hopefully master. Someone once said we were given one mouth and two ears because listening is more important than speaking. I have come to learn that our two eyes also call us to pay attention. Our emphasis should be on listening and paying attention with our ears and eyes. If it were more important to talk than listen, we would probably have two mouths, two heads, one ear and one eye!

A Kind of Beginning

Early February 2022, I started reading *The Confident Woman* by Joyce Meyer. Before I dozed off one night, I underlined and highlighted a paragraph that grabbed my attention:

> "It's important to note that, in many cases <u>successful people have tried many times and failed before they ultimately succeeded.</u> They not only had to **begin with confidence**, they had to **remain confident** when every circumstance seemed to shout at them, Failure! Failure! Failure!" [my underlining and emphasis][2]

I was inspired to collage and look deeper into each of the key ingredients that produce success, that distinguish the extraordinary from ordinary people despite their life mess:

Faith (believe, confidence even when failing or facing challenges) confidence in things hoped for; evidence of things not yet seen (Hebrews 11:1)

Believe (have faith, confidence) to achieve

Courage (embrace the unknown, unfamiliar) not the absence of fear but action in the presence of fear

"God has **used ordinary people to do** amazing, **extraordinary things**. Yet, all of them had to take a **step of faith first**. They had to <u>confidently press forward into the unknown or unfamiliar</u> before making any progress. They had to **believe** <u>they could do</u> what they were attempting to do. **Achieve** comes before **Believe** <u>in the dictionary</u>, but the <u>order is switched in real life</u>." [my underlining and emphasis][3]

The next day, after reading those passages from Joyce Meyer's book, I had to drive to look for some school uniforms for my then four-year-old and get back home to solar installation workers. When we were done uniform shopping, I couldn't be bothered doing a U-turn and going back home the way I knew off the top of my head. It felt easier to punch my address in the GPS instead. I ended up getting completely lost, wasted time and fuel, plus got charged tolls. I was fuming at myself and running my mouth about how it just wasn't my day. There was nothing that could be done about the time lost.

Hearing my annoyance, my daughter consoled me in a very cute way: "Mummy, don't worry, I'll give you some of my piggy bank money because I have lots of it!" At that point we had stopped at an intersection with a ginormous Lorna Jane billboard that looked as if it was almost kind of plonked right in front of me to see. It shut my noisy head and mouth up and stopped me dead in my tracks. It read, 'IT STARTS WITH BELIEVE'.

I couldn't deny that it was almost as if God was calling my attention to be quiet and listen. Others would say it was coincidence, fate, the Universe or whatever they believe in. I knew that I had to park the car somewhere with my little girl, hop out and take a photo of this life-changing lesson to follow through with. Suddenly, the time and money I was thinking I had lost became insignificant and almost seemed worth it for the invaluable lesson I learned. I was so happy to have my daughter with me as it all unfolded. I embraced my imperfect day with a different spirit. My mind and mouth were silenced as I used my eyes and ears to listen.

As we walked back to the car, my little girl chimed in, "I suppose it was a good day after all, Mummy! We must look for a new name for our GPS!" I asked her to do the honours because it did deserve a name. Her response was, "Umm, how about, Believe!" I loved it. Even as we drove back home, and I got another "beep!" as we were hit by yet another toll charge, it didn't hurt as much now. If it took a bit of our fuel and unnecessary toll charges for an almost forty-year-old and a four-year-old to learn an invaluable lesson, then all up, we'd had a good day.

At bedtime, my girl said to me, "Mama, you know Jojo Siwa has a song where she sings – "You believe it; You achieve it!" I was amazed and proud at how deep the teaching had gone down for her. I didn't know it then but asked her to play it for me. The song is called D.R.E.A.M.

By paying attention, listening, and choosing to cut out all the other noise – the day-to-day busyness, all the mess in my life (frustrations, changes, challenges, fears, disappointment) – I went to sleep that day knowing that because I Believe, I will Achieve. It was the same for my daughter.

The possibilities now seemed unlimited ...

BELIEVE & FAITH

BELIEVE to Achieve

Believe – have confidence despite failures or challenges.

FAITH is **confidence** in things hoped –
evidence of things not yet seen.

(the message in Hebrews 11:1)

THE *Mess* HAS THE *Message*

THE CONFIDENT WOMAN
JOYCE MEYER

Now, you might have read the preceding paragraph—about "amazing heights," and thought to yourself, *Yeah, right, Joyce. I'm not able to do anything amazing.* (And I'm scared of heights too. Don't despair if you have thoughts like this. Throughout history, God has used ordinary people to do amazing, extraordinary things. Yet, all of them had to take a step of faith first. They had to confidently press forward into the unknown or unfamiliar before making any progress. They had to believe they could do what they were attempting to do. "Achieve" comes before "Believe" in the dictionary, but the order is switched in real life.

It's important to note that, in many cases, successful people have tried many times and failed before they ultimately succeeded. They not only had to begin with confidence, they had to remain confident when every circumstance seemed to shout at them, "Failure! Failure! Failure!"

10

The D.R.E.A.M song lyrics my daughter told me about got me on a high, like icing on the cake to all I had already learned in my journey, inspiring me to action my own dream: "You can do it if you see it – If you see it, you can be it" … "You just D.R.E.A.M!"

> ♪ **To listen to the song:**
> https://www.youtube.com/watch?v=HJt9xW-2GXI

In mid-2022, I listened to a Steven Furtick sermon about the inspirational songs sung in church, like 'The Blessing'. He says something along the lines of: *The songs are just the soundtrack, your images, your story are the actual movie.*[4]

I now had to turn that dream, that evidence of things not yet seen, into an actual story.

Spirit, Lead Me

> "Are you so foolish? After beginning by means of the Spirit, are you now trying to finish by means of the flesh?" (Galatians 3:3 NIV)

> "At times you find that you start something in faith by the spirit leading you and then at some point you say oh, thank you, God, 'I got it from here' and you pursue it in your own flesh by your own means. The truth though is you end up finding that 'you don't got it' when suddenly there is a plot twist that you don't know how to handle because you didn't write the script in the first place, God did … You manage to buy a house with the spirit leading you, but you will find without the spirit in it, it is not a home but simply just a house."

These words from Steven Furtick[5] ring true to me. The truth is, I have been down this road in the past and still sometimes go down it.

I started writing in a broken home; a place that was no longer a home but just a house, and I searched for the spirit that had led me before.

I have now learned to say, "Spirit, lead me".

I discovered Ariana Berlin, a young gymnast, in a movie I watched called *Full Out*. It's inspired by the true story of her Olympic aspiration that came to a halt when she was in a debilitating car accident. In the movie, Ariana says,

> "We all have our ups and downs, but it's how you deal with them that defines who you are. You must do the thing that you think you cannot do."

Ariana was told that she would never do gymnastics again after her car accident, but she didn't believe them. She chose to believe that she could achieve what she wanted instead.

After her car accident, she first got into breakdancing when she found it hard to do gymnastics, then eventually made it to be part of an accomplished UCLA (University of California, Los Angeles) gymnastics team.

In the movie, Ariana's gymnastics coach said to her, "Sometimes you have to fall before you can fly". This is much like we do as babies before we end up walking. Her physiotherapist also advised her that when you really want something you've got to fight hard for it. If the front door has been slammed in your face, then go via the back door, and if there is none, then go through a window! There is always a way in. It simply takes you choosing to keep on going no matter what. The hurts and disappointments are ironically what build us up, make us strong and who we are. The question is, do you have **faith** strong enough to withstand the seasons? We are taught to walk by faith not by sight, meaning we don't live by our feelings and don't lower our faith to the size of our circumstances.

The foundation for my faith came from the Word in the Bible. The first thing I aim to do each morning is to start with at least a quick reading. Either I read verses directly from my hard copy of the Bible or at times a pop-up verse on my phone. Sometimes my reading triggers a song in my soul and will lead me to a praise and thanks song. 'Spirit Lead Me' is one of my anthems to date.

> ♫ **To listen to the song:**
> https://youtu.be/1Ko4yroBP0A

Spirit Lead Me (by Influence Music and Michael Ketterer)

(Lyrics published here with kind permission)

This is my worship, this is my offering
In every moment, I withhold nothing
I'm learning to trust You, even when I can't see it
And even in suffering, I have to believe it

If You say, "It's wrong," then I'll say, "No"
If You say "Release," I'm letting go
If You're in it with me, I'll begin
And when You say to jump, I'm diving in
If You say, "Be still," then I will wait
If You say to trust, I will obey
I don't wanna follow my own ways
I'm done chasing feelings, Spirit lead me
O Spirit lead me

It felt like a burden, but once I could grasp it
You took me further, further than I was asking
And simply to see You
It's worth it all
My life is an altar
Let Your fire fall

If You say, "It's wrong," then I'll say, "No"
…

Holy (Spirit, Spirit lead me)
Holy Spirit (Holy Spirit, Spirit lead me)
(Yeah, just sing it out, yeah)
O Spirit lead me (Holy Spirit, Spirit lead me)

When all hope is gone and Your Word is all I've got
I have to believe, You still bring water from the rock
To satisfy my thirst, to love me at my worst
And even when I don't remember, You remind me of my worth
I don't trust my ways, I'm trading in my faults
I lay down everything 'cause You're all that I want
I've landed on my knees
This is the cup You have for me
And even when it don't make sense

I'm gonna let Your Spirit lead (Spirit lead me)
I'm gonna let Your Spirit lead (Spirit lead me)
I'm gonna let Your Spirit lead (Spirit lead me)
I wanna let Your Spirit lead (Spirit lead me)

"When your story aligns with God's story, it leads to a Greater Story."

Sam Collier, Hillsong Pastor[6]

In Proverbs, Solomon gave this advice to his son: "Trust in the Lord with all your heart and lean not on your own understanding." (Proverbs 3:5 NIV)

I choose to Listen, Believe and have Faith.

PART 1

Through the Struggles, Challenges, Hurt and Pain

HUMBLE

HUMBLE (or Humility) ≠ thinking less of
yourself = thinking of yourself less

C.S. Lewis

HUMBLE ≠ thinking less of yourself =
thinking of yourself less AND more of others

HUMBLE = less of me and more of him

Bronwen Healy

"Humble yourselves before the Lord,
and he will lift you up."

James 4:10 NIV

Humble is a profound tool –
acknowledging God, **surrendering** our
limited abilities for **his unlimited abilities**

Be completely humble and gentle; be patient,
bearing with one another in love.

Ephesians 4:2 NIV

Instagram Photographer - bartezzz82

My challenges have helped me to discover and understand on a deeper level that being humbled is not just about the day-to-day meaning of experiencing something humbling, that is, going from being on top of the world to being of less importance or nothing; it's much more.

Pray for Me

At the age of eighteen, I had an almost perfect life. I was living in Zimbabwe, preparing to study overseas and begin life alone as an adult. I felt I had freedom and the whole world at my fingertips. Every member of my immediate family was alive and well, then suddenly, my mother passed away in December 2001. This was just over a month before I was to fly out and start what I thought would be my fabulous university life as a teenager in Australia. I could not fully process everything that had just happened in my life then and didn't really grieve at the time, but I didn't realise this back then. It took years for it to finally hit me.

Fast forward fifteen years. I had completed university, started working, and met a guy I thought was tailor-made for me – we had a destination fairy tale wedding, too. We built our dream home in an area that we ironically thought was the kind of place where if you lived there all your problems would just melt away. Our home was completed by the end of 2016, just in time to welcome a new addition to our little family the following year. We seemed like quite the power couple at the time, with all our ducks in a row and our dreams literally coming true one after the other.

It was with the pregnancy that the absence of my mother became more apparent for me. It was by no means a difficult one at all; I was rather blessed in that department. I just simply missed and appreciated my mother a lot more then. Unfortunately, early 2017, my marriage was on the rocks, and this was even more intense just before I gave birth.

I had previously organised a beautiful Gold Coast hinterland babymoon to enjoy the last few weeks out in nature as a couple before welcoming our baby into the world and for us to try to see ourselves as the couple that we were when we first fell in love. The getaway didn't quite go as planned. I initially turned up for it without my plus one. He later came, and we did eventually enjoy the time together. We agreed to try different conflict resolution methods for our issues, but unfortunately our problems continued into the labour and the birth of our beautiful angel.

The naming of our child and how we were to work together going forward from there was like opening a Pandora's box. Our underlying differences – that had always been there – were fully magnified. We tried different modes of communication and resolution to no avail. Due to culture, our marriage had included a bride price ('roora', 'lobola' or dowry), and in the end, I felt forced to consent to his wishes to end our disagreements and move forward.

In my understanding the bride price was a declaration of love not a purchase, but a union of two families. With this conflict it became clear that I had signed up for something I didn't fully get as it was now explained to me that as the groom had paid the bride price it meant for some families that I was marrying into their family values. What about my family upbringing and values? Where did they sit exactly in what I thought was a union, a merging of our two different upbringings? It seemed to me I had to forget who I was and go with the flow of what was ruled out by the family I had married into. It left me feeling confused, misunderstood, broken and emotionally wounded. A wound that my husband didn't understand despite my trying to explain.

It was as if I had willingly but blindly walked into the marriage with eyes wide open. I knew of our spiritual belief differences but had not seen nor quite understood the impact until everything unravelled. My husband was brought up going to Anglican church as well as exposed to Shona (Zimbabwean, African) traditional religion, which I wasn't. Having lost his parents and orphaned as a teenager, as an adult, he had come to believe that the traditional religion was the way to go for him. As he explained to me, this meant in his personal prayer time, instead of praying to Jesus Christ, he engaged in ancestral worship.

I had genuinely not seen the impact of our differences in beliefs coming. There was an added layer that I had only just become aware of. Not only did he practise the traditional religion, but he was also upholding the Zimbabwean Shona traditionalist values from our grandparents' epoch, which have evolved with time. These were very far from my beliefs, how we were when we dated or earlier on in the marriage.

I was now trying to understand my husband, who had metamorphosed into a new person. The way we now dealt with issues or resolved them as a couple was strikingly different from how it had been. I cut myself off from the world. Emotionally and physically, I disconnected from not only my husband at the time but also my family and friends. I had said all I had to in different channels to my husband and no longer had anything else to say, so I shut down. I went mute. What was the point in speaking? No matter what I said or thought, the end result would be that I would just have to consent to my husband's wishes. I was very lost as a wife and mother. I had no idea who I was anymore. It was all a maze for me.

Have you ever felt covered in a thick, dark blanket of sadness with no hope? That's how I felt. I love to laugh, but I had gone for months without it. I remember on one occasion at the hairdresser's, I finally burst out laughing, and literally, as soon as I finished, I felt that blanket of darkness cover me again. Due to my lack of understanding, I struggled with the doctor's diagnosis that I had postpartum depression because I felt it was a cop-out. The issues were not to do with childbirth but marital – the underlying differences in our values and morals, which to me were something separate. Our marriage troubles ended up involving a lot of our family and friends, creating a great deal of noise in our relationship. I couldn't even hear myself think, let alone hear each other's voices as a couple. We lost each other in the noise, and we were broken.

Someone suggested I start counselling on my own even if we couldn't do it as a couple. My husband strongly believed it was all my fault anyway, so I needed to work on it. I eventually started doing it alone, hoping to get myself and the marriage back on track. I decided to work on my emotional wound first and foremost to rebuild emotional and physical intimacy with my husband. At the time, I had no prayer or spiritual life and didn't intend on having one either. When anyone suggested I pray, I asked them to pray for me instead.

Within my marriage I did take some baby steps, actioning what the counsellor advised. I started by working on the lines of communication with my husband, aiming to build myself up again in what now seemed like a new marriage. It was now worlds apart from how we had been for years before that or even how we pictured it at our beautiful destination white wedding or when we created our dream home for our baby.

While I tried to deal with my own struggles, we were still not quite on the same page, as we did not do the counselling together. I worked on implementing the exercises and tools I got from the therapy sessions at home. My husband had his own way of dealing with this new version of us that eventually saw him withdrawing his physical presence from the house and our lives, which killed me. I literally lost my mind trying to balance out the sleepless nights as a new first-time mum, plus the lion's share of care for our child. I felt like a single parent as I found myself for weeks on end without my husband to share the responsibility with as we had done together at the start when he was a hands-on dad. Yes, we had our issues as a couple, but I believed we had to rise above that and continue with our parental duties regardless. Unfortunately, it seemed we had yet another difference in attitude there. Eventually, there was infidelity, which was the straw that broke the camel's back for me.

In July 2017, three months after the birth of our baby, I was certain we were heading our separate ways. Counselling at this later stage was more for my sanity than anything else and to find a way to deal with this new turning point in our lives. To say the whole experience was traumatic and a loss is an understatement. One thing was for sure: we each had our own weaknesses to deal with and address. We needed space to work on them separately and grow to be the best people we could be, first and foremost to enable us to be the best parents for our beautiful daughter, and then to be able to develop other relationships in whatever shape or form.

We encountered many different challenges and battles in that separation to divorce phase. Little did I know that it would painfully drag on for years until 2020. Under Australian law, there must be a year of separation before filing for divorce. In that period, not only did I mourn the loss of my marriage, but I ended up fully realising the loss of my mother. I longed for my mother's touch, simply to cry with my head on her shoulder as I used to and to also express my gratitude to her for being my mother despite the hard times I gave her. It seemed I was back to where I was before I started counselling, if not worse.

More of You Lord and Less of Myself

Before, I felt broken, but this time it seemed I was buried for death. During the marriage separation phase, after another of our many arguments, as we lived under the same roof at the time, I decided to go to church. The first words mentioned as I walked in were, "You are here today because someone has been praying for you". I knew I had previously asked others to do so because I couldn't, so the words felt directed personally to me. This was the start of hearing at least one distinct voice and cutting out the noise from all the rest, including mine. It was the beginning of rebuilding my one-on-one relationship with God. The affirmation that being humble was *more of you Lord and less of me* came to mind. It brought a certain peace to my soul despite the separation turmoil and eventual divorce.

During this period, I had a plethora of feelings creeping in, ranging from thinking less of myself to sadness, low spirit, confusion and anger starting to surface at times. I got an understanding of the meaning behind the song 'Man of Your Word' by Maverick City Music: "If You said it, we believe it,

'Cause You're a man of Your word".

At times we struggle with others keeping their word, but I got to appreciate that there was one man, the Father above, whose word is always constant. He is my salvation and fortress.

> ♫ **To listen to the song:**
> https://www.youtube.com/watch?v=0TrVCZF-4pI

Humans are fickle, but God is constant, loyal, faithful, and so ... *more of him.* The Bible is full of ancient stories of his nature. In the modern day, there is also more of what he has done and is doing for people living in our time. I have referenced these throughout this book.

More of Others and Less of Myself

The mixed bag of confusing feelings I experienced in this period got me to dig even deeper into humility and choose not to think less of myself but think more of others and of myself a little less. On repeat in my head were the words – **HUMBLE – not thinking less of myself but thinking of myself less AND more of others**. By others, I meant whomever I found myself having difficulties with, others in similar situations to me, and above all, God.

As much as I previously had some level of understanding of my part in the marriage breakdown, it took about five years after the divorce to fully understand the effect of my shutting down or silence in our marriage conflict.

A few years after the divorce, I was dating someone when the silent streak struck again. There wasn't much communication at that stage from both ends. I got to understand another layer in the meaning of humility and being humble. It seemed like déjà vu. This time, I experienced it from both sides, but especially from the person I was dating. Experiencing their shutdown mode was a good eye-opener to the impact shutting down or silence can have not only on the relationship but on the other person, too.

If I had to open lines of communication again, with the aim of focusing more on the good of the other person and God despite the situation, I knew I had to be in my best form. I could not control the other person's silence, but I could nip in the bud my shutdown mode. I was now aware I had been down that road before and had to actively do something different about it. I had to remember that it had to be *less of me and more of others*.

A Better Version of Yourself

> There is nothing noble in being superior to others; "true nobility is being superior to your former self".
>
> *Ernest Hemingway*

"Plan to outdo your past, not other people."

Kayla Itsines[7] (Personal trainer, author and entrepreneur)

"Remember you are you own competition. I take daily actions to better myself."

Lisa Messenger[8] (Entrepreneur and author)

What became clear to me is that being humble is not about being inferior to others but about being a better you.

I had to look at how I could do better. When it came to my damaging shutdown mode in relationships, I did try to work on it with conflict resolution, but I didn't completely tackle it in my marriage. However, I tried to improve on this in the later relationship when the same problem arose. It was a challenging but also very educational time for me.

So how did I work on being a better version of myself? Each time I had negative thoughts come through that made me feel less than others, I had a choice to make on how I took action. I consciously redirected my thoughts from the report of **the world**, what it said about me (that is, what was in my head or what others said) to the report of **the Word** and what it said instead. I had to divert my thoughts to not think less of myself but think of myself less and of others more. It was necessary to make good the thoughts I had and focus on what was true and right.

MORE OF YOU LORD: I kept uttering the following quote from the Bible to myself – "… all things work together for good to those who love God, to those who are called to His purpose." (Romans 8:28 New King James Version (NKJV))

MORE OF OTHERS: think of the best of others – in love that protects, trusts, hopes, perseveres. Remembering that love is patient, does not boast, is not proud. Love never fails (1 Corinthians 13).

To force myself to think only of the best of others, I repeated the message I got from the book of Philippians: whatever is True, Noble, Right, Pure, Lovely, Admirable, Excellent and Praiseworthy, think about such things (Philippians 4:8).

I formed thoughts that aligned with all that goodness, be it of others or God, despite what appeared to be bad circumstances.

When it came to thoughts of myself, I repeated the following:

> "4 Rejoice in the Lord always. I will say it again: Rejoice! 5 Let your gentleness be evident to all. 6 Do not be anxious about anything, but in every situation, by prayer and petition, with thanksgiving, present your requests to God. 7 And the peace of God, which transcends all understanding, will guard your hearts and your minds in Christ Jesus … 9 And the God of peace will be with you." (Philippians 4:4-9 NIV)

> "12 … take hold of that for which Christ Jesus took hold of me … Forgetting what is behind and straining toward what is ahead, 14 I press on toward the goal to win the prize for which God has called me heavenward in Christ Jesus." (Philippians 3:12-14)

In my search to humble myself, my spirit led me to BOW,[9] praise and thanks:

Bow – before the Lord with all your cares

Offload – all your angst and humbly hold each thought against the Word of truth

Worship – fix your eyes on him and take your eyes off yourself

Praise and thanks truly are the antidote to anxiety.[10] In this humility journey, there was also a feeling of rejection I struggled with during the marriage breakdown while I was battling to sell the matrimonial home and even when I was learning to walk again on my own. In as much as I began to understand that the **mess** = the **message,** I also got that a **no** in life (rejection) = k**no**wledge.

When people don't see your value, it has nothing to do with your not being good enough. We have got to learn to accept that it is what it is and not internalise rejection. I have come to realise that we need to move our focus on the lessons learned from the experience and make something good, something better for ourselves and ultimately for others also to learn.

I also found solace and peace in the book of Psalms.

"21 I will give you thanks, for you answered me; you have become my salvation. 22 The stone the builders rejected has become the cornerstone." (Psalms 118:21-22 NIV)

I remembered and gave thanks to God for his assurance in saving, finding, and making something of value out of me despite it looking like rejection with my human eyes.

With my heart at ease and peace with the newfound confidence from my humbling experience, I chose more of the Lord and less of myself to channel my challenges into my writing as I let the Peace of God that surpasses all understanding guard and guide me.

TAKEAWAYS

- Don't think less of yourself but think more of others and of yourself less. You can repeat these words like a mantra to help you remember to act this way.

- In challenging situations and conflicts focus more on the **good** side of the other person.

- Take rejection in stride by reminding yourself that a **no** in life is k**no**wledge. You learn from each rejection, and ultimately, others can learn from you.

PEACE

PEACE is not a **physical location** but a **spiritual condition**.

• *Pastor Lia, Heart of God Church*

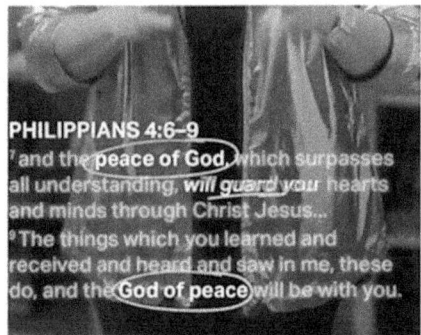

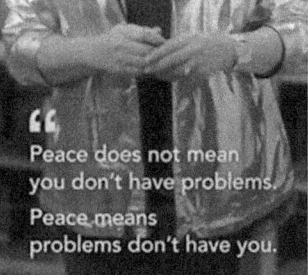

An Uphill Battle

Selling the matrimonial house was complicated from the get-go, and quite literally, singing my praise and worship songs (including 'Defender' by Upper Room, which I mention below) is what brought peace in my chaos. My ex did not hand in his signed paperwork, which was needed to list the house for sale, and a few times left to go overseas, advising that he was never coming back.

I started off 2018 with question marks in terms of how I would manage everything by myself. The house needed both our signatures to sell and that meant I had to go through the court process to get the authority to sell it, having failed to reach any resolution via family relationship centres as my ex declined to attend any meetings. It was not smooth sailing. It took months on end from the 2017 separation discussions to eventually getting the house ready for sale. This was a process that should have taken a week or so, all things being equal.

By early 2018, I was on unpaid parental leave and had to work out how to get the house presentable for sale by myself. It was another tough process, but in the end, I learned a lot. Turfing was one of the big-ticket items to tackle first. I had to work out how to make a super-tight budget fit a project plus balance it all out with the care of an infant.

At the end of April 2018, the first house listing finally went up with the court approval to sell. It was a miracle and a glimmer of hope in the mess. In our consent orders before my ex left the country, the agreement was to sell the house based on values obtained from appraisals. I had thought of selling the house using the initial valuation we had soon after building it, which my ex pointed out was outdated, given that was now over a year ago. My ex, who had dragged out the process of getting any resolution finalised, be it with family centres or court orders, and then further stalled the house sale for months on end as he didn't want to sell, finally gave some good advice to consider. He discouraged me from selling based on the initial valuation and urged me not to let myself be driven by emotions and just sell the house immediately so I could move on. Instead, he suggested doing some market research with professionals.

Based on what seemed like sound advice from my ex, backed by professionals in the industry, I executed the seemingly wise decision not to pursue that initial value or lower. We included a guide of the values to consider in the order agreement, which I followed through with the real estate agent's assessment when we eventually listed the house for sale. A very keen buyer was in the range of the initial value, but I didn't pursue getting this offer in writing due to the latest valuations. Little did I know then that, as they say in real estate, the first offers really are your best. It was a big and tough lesson to learn.

By mid-2018, living separated from my ex under the same roof had its truckload of challenges. What kept me going was other people's support. They alleviated me from 100 per cent care of our child (despite our consent orders clearly stipulating shared responsibility for each parent). On some occasions, I also had different friends help with the house cleaning or maintenance responsibilities, be it mowing or whatever else, as these chores fell on me also. However, my getting help in any way didn't sit well with my ex, and it reached a stage where people were not welcome in our matrimonial home. From childcare to property care and maintenance, I was expected to do it all on my own.

From the outset, I worked blood and sweat to make sure we both maintained a relationship with our daughter. I even enrolled in the family relationship centre course on parenting whilst separated and invited my ex to ensure we at least would be on the same page and do our best with our child. The invite was not taken up.

I also pursued different avenues to spend individual one-on-one time with our child. Initially, my ex welcomed this and implemented it well. However, after a while, he took a step back, though I repeatedly expressed how exhausted I was, even if I wanted to do it all seven days a week.

I began to understand that the parent-child relationship was not something I could enforce or fight for my ex to want to do if he wasn't ready, as that might only be more damaging. Ultimately, it was my ex's responsibility to pursue that accordingly. At some stage, he said he wanted random care days whenever it suited him. I agreed to that initial request but insisted that going forward, it was best to follow through with the agreed days for our child's well-being and to manage our relationships better. That didn't sit well with my ex, and he advised that he would seek alternative arrangements formally, which I agreed to as well, considering he was unwilling to take up the existing care plan. Until he was ready, I had to put my big girl pants on and deal with it. I needed to dig deep to be available 100 per cent for the care of our daughter, be it financially or physically, despite my exhaustion from all the property responsibilities.

Occasionally, it felt like we'd had a breakthrough in selling the house as per the valuation price with interested parties that inspected it more than once and had private viewings during the week. However, each time when all seemed lined up for a sale, for whatever reason, it fell through. Prospective buyers would be turned off by the new builds in the new estate, the shooting range or the highway. This was despite there being a wall along the estate, with our house being a fair distance away. It was separated from everything by a bit of bush and a row of other houses. Not to mention that our house had met the wall and window acoustic standards for noise levels.

I had meticulously gone through vendor feedback to work on items that were within my power to action, such as sanding all the downstairs wooden floors, as some areas had scratches or whatever else. I checked in with the agents based on their experience and the selling strategy in place. All seemed in order and in line with the other houses being sold in the estate, so I followed their lead, together with the consent orders. All of it was to no avail, though.

Living separated from my ex under the same roof brought on challenges that impacted not only the living but also the selling conditions. After getting pressure from my ex to change agents when the first three-month campaign did not achieve the offer price we had agreed the house was worth, I ended up hiring a second agent who believed they could drive up the price with their strategies. The agent didn't think going ahead with an auction at the start of the campaign was advisable, so I went with their expert advice. They were going to gauge the market with regular house openings first.

About a month into the new campaign, the agent felt uncomfortable due to my ex's intimidating behaviour and threats to block a scheduled inspection. They refused to go ahead with any further house inspections, stating

I needed to alert the police. My ex had his own beliefs about how the agent should go ahead with the selling strategy. I tried to inform the agent that I could relate to how they felt, but despite my convincing them that I had the court authorisation for them to carry on as planned, they were simply uncomfortable doing any further work at that stage. I got the local authorities to intervene – their speed to respond and address our issue was like a miracle – and my ex ended up stepping aside.

After this, the agent seemed to go ahead with the auction a little earlier than they initially advised, despite my asking them to follow their initial plan. I even double-checked if they were now doing so because they felt uncomfortable after the previous encounter with my ex when he tried to pressure them to follow a certain selling strategy. They assured me that was not the case. The auction went ahead, but unfortunately, there were no registered bids. One buyer did come sometime after with an offer about $70k (AUD) less than the initial verbal offer we got in the first campaign, much lower than I even initially thought of selling the house prior to the agreement orders. My ex and I had ended up on the same page about the valuation and worth of the house as per our consent orders and that offer was nowhere near what we had agreed on or believed it would sell for at the time.

Unfortunately, we didn't realise that the sale was going to be a long uphill battle. With the house taking longer to sell came all sorts of blame. My ex now believed I was intentionally not selling it, yet I had faithfully kept at it all the way through. I was still unwaveringly cleaning up after my ex and giving even more deep cleans after his parties. I kept up with the regular house maintenance plus anything that was broken since it all still fell on me to ensure the house was in display home mode for inspections. I was committed to putting in the best work with each campaign I had with a real estate agent from end to end, following their lead on what they advised was the best strategy to pursue the selling price range both my ex and I had agreed on.

I was now back at work at that stage and had to cover the full mortgage, which I knew I couldn't keep up with for too long, but I had hope of a sale within the year.

After failing to sell with the next campaign, I found myself facing a court date from my ex. It was regarding breaching the house sale via the house pricing and not accepting or encouraging the initial offer in the first campaign. (As a reminder, this was in the range that he had discouraged me from considering pricing or selling the house for.) I was the one who was given the court authority to sell, so ultimately, the responsibility was mine, and I was answerable. Although I had followed the order agreement to a tee, a seed of doubt was planted in my mind, so I was now anxious.

Finding Peace from Anxiety

I wanted the loop I was stuck in to stop because it seemed like one challenge and failure after another on repeat. A wise man says, focus on circumstances and the pain becomes more unbearable. This was the case for me when I ended up in depression. Peace was indeed not my physical location[11] (our beautiful matrimonial dream home had become a battleground), and I had to work on my spiritual condition.

To regain hope and peace in the middle of it all, I reminded myself of the word of God, which gives peace that surpasses all understanding, and I sought it in every way possible. I looked for ways to wear that peace and not the spirit of fear through reading, prayer, song, other people's stories, church sermons and my support network. I found that changing the focus to singing (praise and worship) or reading (the Word) gave me peace in the middle of my problems. (This is what I did, but perhaps you prefer to change the focus to drawing, writing or painting). Through shifting my focus, my spirit somehow ended up at peace at the height of my storms.

In a TV sermon, Dr Charles Stanley says that 'peace' in Greek = to bind together, and so when he thinks about the peace of God, we are bound together with him, in his presence and power.[12]

When we can thank him, the anxiety crumbles within us, and peace prevails. Nothing else may have changed physically, but an overwhelming sense of indescribable peace comes from an intimate relationship with Jesus Christ.

Dr Charles questions what the wisest thing to do is when you go through trauma. Do you get out the bottle and drink/smoke/chew/have an affair/run away from circumstances? What is your response?

When you turn to the Lord Jesus Christ, you may not even know what to say at first or know how to pray. It's okay – He knows your heart. Just talk to him. Before long, you will be praising God because that's the work of the Holy Spirit, to mellow up our hearts and give us understanding so that we see He is willing.

"Do not be anxious about anything, but in every situation, by prayer and petition, with thanksgiving, present your requests to God". (Philippians 4:6 NIV)

Does this mean you can live anxiety-free? No, because sometimes we are hit with anxiety immediately. But when I turn to the Lord and start praying and thanking him, God meets my anxiety, and it turns to peace. When I am anxious, I thank him that he is in control, knows better, knows my future and works it all out even though I don't understand it, don't like it and it hurts terribly. I thank God that he hasn't left me to myself and that he will help me through this.

The Power of Singing

Singer Steffany Gretzinger[13] says at times you sing because you believe you are sure, and at times you sing until you are sure. On my journey I have bounced between these two conditions, but one thing is for sure, each time it brought me peace.

When I started singing, I was depressed, lonely and confused about what my marriage meant. I had been hit by the infidelity whirlwind and was trying to find a way out of it all, for the hurt to just stop. The song 'Even When It Hurts' (and Psalm 69:29-32) was one of my staples at the height of my marriage turmoil. I sang it almost every morning with one relative who had the most angelic voice and was certainly one of my earthly angels. She supported me physically, emotionally and spiritually almost every day in the earlier stages of my struggles. Just singing together brought about unexplainable harmony, even though nothing was right at that point. At times I would sing it out loud on my own with tears rolling down my cheeks in pain, then sometimes it would be with joy and peace in my heart despite the turmoil. Taya Smith, singer in 'Even when It Hurts' (by Hillsong United) starts off with Psalm 69 from the book of Psalms:

> "29 I'm hurt and in pain.
> Give me space for healing, and mountain air.
> 30 Let me shout God's name with a praising song,
> Let me tell his greatness in a prayer of thanks.
> 31 For God, this is better than oxen on the altar,
> Far better than blue-ribbon bulls.
> 32 The poor in spirit see and are glad—
> Oh, you God-seekers, take heart!"
> (69:29-32 The Message (MSG))

She moves on to say that no matter what you are facing, God's praise should be on your lips. If you have been doing life long enough, you will find that, at times, there are awesome seasons where it feels like you are on the mountaintop and it's easy to praise God, and there are other times when it's a sacrifice to do so. (For God, as per the book of Psalms, such a sacrifice is far better than a material one – oxen, bulls and the like). The prayer is that we will praise God no matter what is happening around us – we will praise God and that will be the sound coming off our lips – *even when it hurts*.

> ♫ **To listen to the song and read the lyrics:**
> https://youtu.be/ByM53v4JauY
> https://hillsong.com/lyrics/even-when-it-hurts-praise-song/

Peace Is Your Power

At a church service I attended, a lady named Varsity shared her story of finding peace in turbulent times. She had faith that God would guide her through, and she spoke of the following Bible passage:

PEACE

"Anyone who loves me will obey my teaching ... the Holy Spirit, whom the Father will send in my name, will teach you all things ..." (John 14:23-26 NIV)

Varsity and her husband were on their two-day babymoon in Byron Bay, Australia, when her husband received a redundancy call. It was unexpected, and Varsity was about to go on parental leave, so she was now anxious about how they would provide for their baby. Next, Varsity got gastro and had to go to the hospital. On their way from Byron Bay, their car tyre burst, and so did the tears (they certainly would if this were me). Both she and her husband were useless at changing tyres, and at that stage, her peace was out the window. She had to learn that *His peace is your power,* and if you allow him, he will give you peace. Through her Bible readings and reflection, she explored peace and found her spirit at rest and empowered by it. She shared some of what she discovered.

The book of John 14:27 continues, "Peace I leave with you; My peace I give you. I do not give to you as the world gives. Do not let your hearts be troubled and do not be afraid." (NIV)

Even amid drama, you will find his peace and calmness. Even with everything around you breaking down, going crazy and nothing going right, the peace of God says, *I got this, don't worry, it's under control,* and you can find internal calmness. People often make it more about what is going on externally. In the book of Mark, Jesus told his disciples to get on a boat so they could go to the other side of the lake. They got caught up in a storm and water started filling the boat. Jesus, who was on board, was fast asleep through all this drama. The disciples woke Jesus up, concerned that he didn't care about them perishing. Jesus calmed the storm with three words – "Peace! Be still!" – then asked why they were afraid and if they still had no faith. (4:35-41 ESV)

Being in the will of God does not mean it's all going to be peaches and cream. Sometimes we make choices to avoid and escape the drama, yet that is what helps us mature and shapes us to be who we are today, and we should learn to embrace it. God will give peace during that drama. Our position is to check in and question why we are afraid and if we still have faith, we need to work on that.

Varsity learned to work on her internal calmness via the word of God despite her chaotic world.

"Peace is a gift from God designed to empower you.

His Peace, Your Power."

Varsity

The message says *Peace. Be still* – "The LORD will fight for you; You need only to be still." (Exodus 14:14 NIV)

The evening I got the email serving me court documents for breaches of the house sale, I had to pull out that morning's Word of the day to focus on it and stop my mind flipping out. Without that inner peace that Varsity shared, I could see my confidence chipping away slowly but surely, and I would be standing there with no faith.

"Do not worry about anything, instead, <u>pray about everything</u>. <u>Tell God what you need and thank him for all he has done</u>. Then you will <u>experience God's peace</u>, which exceeds anything we can understand. <u>His peace will guard your hearts and minds</u> as you live in Christ Jesus." [My emphasis] (Philippians 4:6-7 New Living Translation (NLT))

I reflected on everything that had happened in relation to the house sale so far. Being thankful for the fact that I eventually got the house listed for sale in the first place brought back a sense of peace. Then I recalled how, as I waited for the court's authorisation to sell the house, I had seen God's goodness with the initial agent I listed with. They helped me out on their own time with some house maintenance, like painting walls, which they advised needed freshening up to present the house in the best light. It was all mind-blowing, considering at the time I was living mostly on pre-pregnancy savings, and really, in a way, they hired themselves to be my free painters.

There was also my support network, which I mentioned earlier, of course.

PEACE

And I remembered seeing the same goodness as I filed my Family Court paperwork to get the house up for sale when they pointed me in the direction to get the best help. The court admin staff were professional and helpful in processing my application. There were no delays in my court session, and I got the authorisation for sale.

I now stood in prayer for a positive outcome to the new court case for breaches of the house sale. I gave the chaos, the mess in my life, to God in prayer in exchange for peace. I came across a message that said:

> "God's plan is always best; sometimes the process is painful and hard but don't forget … he is doing something great for you! He will turn pain into peace; heartbreak into honour."
>
> *Anon*

As I wore that peace, my physical condition didn't change. In fact, it seemed to be headed from bad to worse! But my spiritual condition certainly was changing enough for me to face the myriad challenges that seemed to come down on me like a ton of bricks. Acknowledging the good through thanks and praise with the Lord as my defender gave me the peace to put me at ease as I kept growing.

As I mentioned above, the song 'Defender', by Upper Room, was my go-to song in this period. One of the lines is, "Your love becomes my greatest defence".

> ♫ **To listen to the song:**
> https://www.youtube.com/watch?v=Za-yGR3sbNw

Through all my struggles I also found my strength in the book of Psalms, Psalm 29, by David:

> "… ascribe to the Lord glory and strength … the glory due his name … The Lord sits enthroned over the flood" [for me the challenges or

struggles at times appeared to be like floods in my life where I felt I was sinking].

"… The Lord gives strength to his people, the Lord blesses his people with peace" [in my heart this drew me back to the gospel (Mark 4:35-41) mentioned earlier when the disciples' boat was sinking in a storm and all Jesus had to say to calm the storm was, "Peace! Be still!"]. (Psalms 29 NIV)

I read the words from this Psalm during the floods and storms in my life and looked to him to give me peace.

Takeaways

- Remember, even if you can't change your physical condition, you can change your spiritual condition and find inner peace.

- Move your focus away from difficult circumstances through music, praise and worship. Try reading, singing, painting, drawing, writing – whatever creative form brings you peace.

- Your peace is your power – it will help you battle anxiety and face life's challenges.

- Be thankful for the good in the chaos – it will give you peace.

- I believe in God to work on my spiritual condition and for those who also believe: Peace of God will guide you. God of Peace will guard you.

PART 2

THROUGH THE WALK

CONFIDENCE & PATIENCE

Faith is **CONFIDENCE** in things hoped for –
evidence of things not yet seen.

(the message taken from Hebrews 11:1)

"But if we hope for what we do not see, we wait for it with patience."

Romans 8:25 (ESV)

PATIENCE = *hupomone* (Greek) – spiritual endurance. Hanging on despite great trials and sufferings.

bibletools.org

Instagram Photographer - bartezzz82

"… imitate those who through faith and patience inherit what has been promised."

Hebrews 6:11-13 (NIV)

Instagram Photographer - bartezzz82

Evidence of Things Not Seen

One of my friends sent me a reading that opened me up more to the unseen and what we hope for. It led me down a path of faith, confidence and patience that was packed with new discoveries. I was at the peak of my 2019 house-selling struggles and ongoing challenges with no end in sight. I had clocked a year and moved into a second, taking the house off and on the market, then unsuccessfully trialling different agents' strategies. I even tried selling on my own, which is not so popular in Australia, but an owner-selling agency believed this was the point of difference. I gave it a good go with zero bites.

After that, I wound up with yet another realtor, as it seemed they were still the way to go in the Australian context. He collaborated very closely with me, doing much more than what the other agents offered with each inspection. The Frank Property team went beyond being agents, becoming colleagues for life, not only with the big-ticket items but even the small or what might have appeared that way. For example, at the end of an inspection, we would thank each other in our mother tongue. The realtor, on behalf of his team, would say *tinotenda* ('thank you' in Shona and a trick to remember my daughter's name – hope, believe, faith, trust). I would then respond with a 'thank you' in Mandarin, saying *xie xie*, which I learned should sound approximately like the 'sie' in 'Sienna': 'sie sie', when you say it quickly.

Anyway, I had another one of the many house sale inspections after paying top dollar for the front-page online listing with fresh professional photos plus a short video to help stand out. We even advertised on some Chinese platforms. The house price was left open for the market to set this time, and there was hope.

As always, I had taken the time to immaculately present the house like a display home yet again. I pulled late nights and early mornings at the expense of losing a chunk of the weekend, plus quality time with my daughter. Every now and then we would have an opening during the week, too. For each inspection I would faithfully put the bread-crumb trail of house sale road signs leading to our house from the estate road entrance.

After all that effort resulted in a loud silence from potential buyers, my spirit was low. It wasn't the first time I'd had a day with no traffic, but on one particular day, I just felt worn out by this long, winding tunnel. Before our usual goodbye, I asked my realtor what else we could do. They assured me that all that could strategically or physically be done was in order. Their ultimate answer before leaving was simply – 'keep the faith'. It sounded so cliché, and depending on my attitude, it could have been the most useless advice or the best. Of course, at this stage I knew deep down that they were right. But without seeing when the sale was going to happen or when things were going to change for me, I just had so many unanswered questions and didn't know what else to do. All I was left with were their parting words ringing in my ears – keep the faith.

A girlfriend came over later that day. She found me at midday in my enormous ensuite bedroom with block-out blinds, curtains all closed, in bed covered with my blankets from head to toe for good measure. It is funny in hindsight, but that was indeed one of my darkest moments. I did have my Bible somewhere close to me as I had hoped to get a word from it to keep the faith. Perhaps like I had heard from others' stories it would fall open to the exact reading that would speak directly to my situation, but that hadn't quite been the case on that day. As soon as my friend opened the door, she quickly exclaimed how sad and dark it was in there. She was spot on. The state of the room described exactly how I felt at that moment.

One of the devotional readings my friend forwarded me later was by writer and speaker Alicia Bruxvoort[14] from the book of Romans:

> "But if we hope for what we do not see, we wait for it with patience." (Romans 8:25 ESV)

What we hope for requires not just faith and confidence but also patience. Alicia highlights that the original word for 'patience' used in the book of Romans 8:25 is *hupomone*, which relates to endurance, a person holding on, persevering and refusing to give up with that 'hang-in-there power'.

That is what I needed to dig into further and grasp.

CONFIDENCE & PATIENCE

Confidence, faith and patience go together. At that stage without a doubt my spiritual eyes, those deep down inside, saw a brighter future, which was currently unseen in the physical. This hope I had for what I did not see in the physical world was my challenge. My confidence and faith in a better tomorrow despite the current today was grounded in the promises I got from the word of God, but this was clearly a lesson I needed to expand more on and exercise.

I once saw an interesting clip on human behaviour and how our natural selves know how to reach our higher goals, but somehow, we fail to get there as we are. The presenter talked about how we need to redesign our internal selves first. In my experience, this equated to the work I needed to do to change the design of my spirit and build up that patience (spiritual endurance) to keep hanging on no matter what and reach my goal.

In Alicia Bruxvoort's story, the clarification for me came from her little girl. She was having a make-believe tea party and wanted to use a tea set from her mother's kitchen. Her mother had promised to get it for her from the top shelf after she had finished her laundry. The little girl was excited, thanked her mother and waited for her in the kitchen. A little while later, there was the sound of shattering ceramic and wailing. Her daughter, in tears, apologised, then explained how she got tired of waiting, didn't think her mum was going to keep her promise, and she now wished she had just been patient. Alicia realised that her daughter wanted to trust her word but had no patience, no fortitude to see it fulfilled. It was glaringly obvious from her little girl's actions that she was getting a reminder, and to be frank, so was I.

Faith is confidence in what we hope for, evidence of the unseen that gives the courage and determination to trust the word of God, and patience is what gives the staying spirit to trust in his time, not ours.

However, at times even when we are doing our best, it seems we are getting nowhere fast. In Angus Buchan's story and the movie based on his life, *Faith Like Potatoes*, we see the condition for a miracle is difficulty and for a great miracle is impossibility. Angus had already faced an avalanche of personal toil and loss but was on the verge of losing his farm to the bank. Although scientists had warned farmers not to plant at that time of year unless they had irrigation due to the drought, against everyone else's beliefs, Angus believed that planting potatoes in that season was what he was meant to do. He went ahead with his plan and planted them in the dry dust. He kept his faith, and at harvest time, it was a bumper harvest. He went on to feel and smell the potatoes, saying that our faith in God should be like that, like potatoes.

Without great trials, our faith is often unseen.

> "To learn strong faith is to endure great trials."
>
> *George Mueller*

As simply as my realtor had put it, I had to 'keep the faith' – to have the staying spirit, I needed to do the internal work. My support system played a major role in providing me with resources, but I had to find ways to do some work on a personal level. I figured to have a kind of 'hang-in-there' attitude, you've got to have faith, belief, trust, and confidence in something.

Believing in Miracles

In my search for spiritual rest despite my physical location – I learned peace, rest, surrender to God on another level through fasting (note: you can do this in different ways. I will elaborate below). It built on my confidence to hang on. No matter what happened in 2019, it would be what God the Father's aerial view of my life saw as the best way forward. I had to trust the process. I made a promise to myself or a pact with him to trust in him, in the now and in the future, no matter what and especially if the result looked very dark from a human viewpoint. My identity was rooted as a child of God.

Further to that I chose to remind myself of the meanings of the names that were in and around me, that reiterated who I was and what I had to aim for. Tinotenda, Ruvimbo – I had to be thankful, believe, trust, hope and have faith in the Lord. Kudzai – give glory, praise, respect, honour the Lord. Arianah – very holy – lioness, heart of God. And a name from my support network, Mwari Haatsari – God doesn't choose.

CONFIDENCE & PATIENCE

I had confidence that God is very holy, the best and excellent, that I am his lioness arising, his heart, his love. He did not choose with the miracles we read about in the Bible, nor does he choose with those he performs for people who live in our time. I had faith he would pull off one of his biggest ones yet, despite what seemed like a never-ending winter. I sang the song '(God of) Miracles' (see below) even when my soul told me otherwise, or my circumstances seemed bleak.

> "So often as believers we want to blame God when something goes wrong, but the truth is, God's good, God's faithful. Just because our circumstance change that doesn't mean those truths change."
>
> *Chris Quilala*

I learned 'Miracles' is a song by Chris Quilala and his wife after the loss of their child. They had believed in a miracle, which didn't happen the way they hoped. After their loss, it was important for them to keep the truth of God as the risen one in front of them, to hang on to this belief, and so they started their song writing. Alyssa Quilala said that on 1 December 2014, life asked her the hardest question she had ever had: Will you trust God in the midst of trauma and loss?

The question for you is, will you trust God or whatever your superpower is in the middle of your deepest, darkest problems?

From the book of John: "I have told you these things, so that in me you may have peace. In this world you will have trouble. But take heart! I have overcome the world." (John 16:33 NIV)

Of course, my challenges were different from those of Chris Quilala and his wife with the loss of their child. I could not (and still cannot) even imagine what that would be like. Our suffering came from different sources, but no matter the size or cause, I knew that I could relate to their pain in my suffering and that in our crying, our tears were the same. My life had appeared to go in the opposite direction from what I had dreamed of. All I knew is I wanted that confidence, courage and peace that Jesus talked about as one who had overcome the world, that which enabled Chris to stand and sing with his wife after the death of their child:

"I believe in you

You're the God of Miracles."

Chris and Alyssa's story and the book of John spoke volumes to me at the time. For me, this meant that by believing in the Easter miracle story and the power of the Holy Spirit that resurrected Jesus, the only son who defied all human odds and defeated death, the one thing man cannot, I could have peace. He overcame the world. My accepting this did not mean I wouldn't have trouble. Jesus himself said, "In this world you will have trouble" (John 16:33 NIV). But I had to take heart, have courage, and hang on to the Word, the Spirit, with that 'hang-in-there power'. Trouble had nothing on me; I would overcome it.

> ♫ **To listen to the song and hear the full story behind it:**
> https://youtu.be/eOjOT1GpxsA

God's Hand at Work

In early 2019, I was still living under the same roof as my ex in an unhealthy environment psychologically. Some of my family informed me they had received threats concerning what my not selling the house meant and were not comfortable with our living situation. They constantly checked in on me. The periods in between were at times truly a haze, and I remember a couple of moments I thought God had a bad sense of humour, sitting on his throne, having a good laugh at me. In hindsight, as I reflect on the events that occurred, including the way my ex carefully cherry-picked evidence for the executed court case against me for not pursuing the initial house offer or supposedly not working with the agents to sell the house, God was for me.

My ex put his case against me so eloquently, and he was so good at gaslighting me, even I started to find his case believable and couldn't comprehend how I could have messed up and gone against what was agreed not only in the consent orders but in outside talks before, during and after with my ex and all the relevant professionals. Nevertheless, I chose to hand in the full picture of all the correspondence from end to end for each of the examples that had been picked for the court case, then left the rest to God and the judge in the driver's seat to decide in the Federal Circuit and Family Court. In the end, with further escalations of our inconducive living environment, the police ended up also lodging a case with the Magistrates Court on my behalf for psychological and emotional abuse.

As I faced multiple court rounds, I was at peace with my confidence rooted in God for each matter. Although these events had made me question God's sick sense of humour, the rulings were in my favour, and rather than being the beginning of my downfall, brought about a change in my circumstances for the better. I literally saw his hand with the final decision where I was entrusted with even more responsibilities for the house sale, as opposed to being stripped of them, which had been the initial reason for the court case. I was given power of attorney to finalise all the sale paperwork with the bank, too, when the house sold.

Not only that, I was granted more than I thought to even ask for as the Family Court also gave me sole occupancy. This was part of the result of the court case in which I was found to be non-negligent in breaching the house sale order.

I was deeply grateful to have seen God's hand at work in my life.

As the property court case wrapped up, the one for psychological and emotional abuse opened. Similar to the property case, what had begun as a campaign against me led to a positive result for me. I was granted a protection order with both court decisions requesting that my ex leave the house for it to be sold.

I have got to say that the emotional and psychological turmoil at times felt like I was in an actual physical boxing rink with a heavy-weight champion. At my worst, I was a woman in her mid-thirties, 160 centimetres (around 5 foot 2 inches) tall, who had lost about 20 kilograms and weighed about 40 kilograms (around 88 pounds), a weight I once was in my mid-teens. As an adult woman, I was literally a moving skeleton. I was facing a much taller and heavier man than me, who was at least double my weight then. He kept throwing around these heavy emotional and psychological punches that felt so real, they took me down with the biggest of thuds.

When I was down, I felt so weak and like I was just hanging by a thread. I was desperately crawling not on my knees but my tummy in the murkiest of waters with the little bit of strength I had left just to keep going and survive. If it were real-life boxing, you would just be wondering, why doesn't she simply give up? Because what's going to happen is obvious, and it seems stupid to keep trying to fight back.

It didn't seem like there was any hope for me. I didn't have a snowball's chance in hell of winning the fight. Why even bother fighting when it was clearly a losing battle? I have since learned that I am a stern believer in better die trying than not do anything at all, even when the odds seem stacked against you.

It was a roller coaster ride with the law for a while, with all this happening before it was addressed, recognised or known by many as coercive control. There was no physical evidence, and so it was especially difficult to say, even to myself, that it was abuse since there was no 'hole in the wall' as someone in authority once said to me. It did bring me to the realisation back then that there was a hole in the system because at times, and unfortunately for some, the hole is six feet under by the time the law intervenes.

With my experience with my ex, among other driving forces, one of my long-time friends and I had started some groundwork in 2018 on JDE foundation to play our part in covering that gap. Unfortunately, about a year and a half later, there was a young lady, Hannah Clarke, and her three kids, who ended up losing their lives. It was very unfortunate that it took these four lives for the law to change and for a better understanding or awareness of coercive control.[15]

My story was different, and I am forever grateful.

After the court cases, I now had somewhat of a clean slate to sell the matrimonial house as a sole occupant. At this stage, the aim was just to get a written contract not necessarily based on the bank valuation or real estate agents' appraisals.

In all honesty, knowing the truths based not only on the Bible stories but those of people in my time, plus my very own experiences, did not mean I didn't face dark and stormy days. With the hardships of being back at work, aiming to keep up with the full mortgage repayments, financial and physical care of a toddler, plus immaculately presenting the house for sale every weekend for most weekends in 2019 and it not moving – the non-sale was especially now getting to me. It seemed the market did not find the house attractive for a myriad of reasons, and those who did were possibly aware of its age by then. The couple who put in verbal offers were offering peanuts that would not only leave the mortgage owing but also other out-of-pocket expenses, such as payments to the realtor, lawyers, government, and other bank fees. It just made no sense. I had no way to fund that difference out of pocket, plus I would have nothing to divide up. I wouldn't have anything left to find somewhere new to live with my daughter.

Finding Hope in the Dark

Towards the end of 2019 there seemed to be hope of a sale and the realtor encouraged two interested buyers to put their best offers in writing as that was the main game plan this time around. They wanted some time with the December-January holidays coming up, and the realtor suggested wrapping up the campaign and then commencing a new one in the new year. It all seemed so close and yet so far without a written contract. I would at times find myself again slipping back into that dark space.

However, I now knew of tools to use to deal with the depression. I had the greatest support system: colleagues, neighbours, family and friends who supported me, and this time I took their help on board. I didn't choose to hide in my hole. I was given pretty dresses to wear when I did step out of the house, so I looked and felt good about myself, as well as flowers and the like. They did random check-ins and tea dates. Throughout the process I got help physically with cleaning for inspections, pickups, drop offs and even babysitting when I had inspections or just needed a break from it all to deal with my mental and physical health so that I could be there for my toddler.

Some gave me financial gifts or loans. This came from my family, friends and even surprisingly from the legal help I got from a barrister I didn't even know before then. Back at work they supported a work-life balance with my change in situation. I realised how there were people or angels on Earth who were there for me at different times for different reasons. I believe God gave them grace to be there for me in my time of need. After I was out of that situation, some of their situations changed and I realised that I, too, could be in a position to be of help to them or others in whatever form.

In my time of need, I had those who continually stood and encouraged me spiritually with prayer, readings and worship. I saw God's hand cover me with these angels in every area of my life. I followed through with the therapy I had started during the postnatal phase. I also forged my own relationship with God via the church family support who helped feed my spiritual being. I dug deep into that one-on-one relationship with my heavenly Father. I was loved by all around me. I found myself in an extremely fortunate and blessed position covered by these angels on Earth in every area of my life – physically, mentally, financially, emotionally and spiritually.

I also took up a lot of reading – inspirational, self-help or self-development books, and I journalled my journey as I sought to find the beauty in the unexpected good or bad, as well as the associated learnings.

One of the books in my collection provided me with seven secrets of confidence. Love is one of the secrets that Joyce Meyer refers to in *The Confident Woman*.[16] She points out how knowing that you are loved is important, and knowing the love is from someone you can trust gives you a comforting feeling. God will not only love us as such but also provides people who will, and when he does, Joyce encourages us to be sure to remain thankful for those people.

I am very grateful for all my angels as I was surrounded and covered by love, and I could keep going no matter what I faced: "… perfect love drives out fear" (1 John 4:18 NIV).

Using the Tools at Hand

I eventually got to learn that when my spirit is low, I need to dig deeper to find peace – meditating on the Word, reading or writing helped. In a later chapter I will elaborate a bit more on my writing, my gratitude and especially my 30-day journalling. If you can't change your circumstances, then change yourself, and I found journalling the good or things to be grateful for certainly changed me.

Whatever it is I could do, that is what I did, and I ran with that. At times I also included fasting as I zoomed in on reading, praying, reflection for action, praise and worship. It was a good way to work towards that peace to boost my confidence and patience tank.

After a year of recovery, when my ex was no longer living under the same roof, and I was physically, emotionally and psychologically healthier, I sought a breakthrough via fasting. With the help of different professionals, I started a three-day fast in December 2019 to feed my spirit, and even though no sale happened, my spirit moved. I decided to keep the three-day fast as a habit once a month instead of once a year or in a blue moon, and I still do it in some form to date.

I realised whenever my spirit seems uneasy or low, fasting helps bring back peace to keep that confidence and patience going. The initial fast I did was the three-day Esther fast (just water or tea (no milk)), and I did this fast as I read the Esther story I talk about just below. I came to a personal realisation that just as I feed my physical being food and exercise, fasting and reading the Bible feed my spiritual being to keep me going.

Fasting can consist of different ways or things for people based on their different life situations, so please do seek advice from professionals depending on the type of fasting you decide to pursue. It could be abstaining from food until a certain time of the day (mostly 3 p.m. for me) or staying away from social media for a certain period or staying off wine for a month (which I sometimes do) and the like to use that time for some quiet time to work on your spirit. I find myself spiritually and mentally healthier after fasting, as I focus on my inner being. I gain a certain clarity on whatever it is I am dealing with internally and find the tools I need to cope with anything going on externally as well.

In the story of Esther, she sent this message to Mordecai:

"Go, gather together all the Jews who are in Susa, and fast for me. Do not eat or drink for three days, night or day. I and my attendants will fast as you do. When this is done, I will go to the king, even though it is against the law. And if I perish, I perish." (Esther 4:16 NIV)

As I had my own fast, reading this strengthened the prayer time and gave me hope, courage and confidence to face whatever was coming my way. The same courage and confidence that Esther exuded, though she knew that after her prayer and fast, she would face the king to try and save the Jewish people and risked perishing if he did not welcome her presence.

It's almost as if with the fast and the clarity it brings, whatever we then go ahead and do, even if we do not get our expected result, then there will be a peace about it as God is in control and "we know that in all things God works for the good of those who love him". (Romans 8:28 NIV)

As the story of Esther unfolds, Mordecai is honoured by the Lord, though Haman sought to kill him and all Jews. The king discovered Haman's plan, so they impaled Haman on the pole he had so carefully set up for Mordecai (Esther 7:10). Then the king's fury subsided.

It's just like Psalm 23 says, "The Lord is my shepherd … You prepare a table before me in the presence of my enemies". (Psalms 27:1-5 NIV) Whatever enemies we have, God will deal with them, so all is well. At times, the enemies we face come from within us and in other cases, they come from outside. God is with us, either way, to lead us as our shepherd.

With all the Lord had done for me, especially but not limited to what he did in all the court sessions, I stood more aware and more able than previous years to look for ways to fix my eyes on Jesus. My aim was (and still is) to consciously speak and listen to the Holy Spirit, God as he speaks from his holy place.

CONFIDENCE & PATIENCE

I pretty much saw events in my life align with how they unfolded for Esther and Mordecai. Esther got favour from God and the king as he welcomed her when she presented herself, and her requests were granted to save and stand for the Jews. As did Mordecai, who continued to refuse to honour Haman by standing up against him despite his threat to destroy all Jews. Not only was Mordecai's enemy destroyed but he was also given the king's signet ring that Haman had worn, plus his estate. Mordecai was now second in power to the King of Iran and given the authority to save the Jews. It was favour upon favour and the tables were turned, with the destruction of those who had been out to destroy them.

All this reminded me of the start of the song 'Raise a Hallelujah' by Bethel Music.

> ♫ **To listen to the song:**
> https://www.youtube.com/watch?v=awkO61T6i0k

The story of a little boy called Jaxon and his fight for survival through his health challenges is told by Jonathan David Helser, one of the singer-songwriters.

Jaxon was airlifted to intensive care a few days before Christmas and a symphony of prayer rose to heaven in the form of this song. A couple of weeks into the fight, a text came through saying that they didn't think Jaxon would make it through the night. The musician says he felt 'a giant of unbelief' stand in front of him and didn't think they would see a miracle. As that giant stood in front of him, this song then started pouring out: "I raise a Hallelujah! In the presence of my enemy, I raise a Hallelujah! Louder than the unbelief!"[17]

The giant of unbelief then just started falling. The community sang this one note in prayer for the little boy's miracle and survival story (Jaxon was in the audience when David told this story). That giant regretted the day that he ever pointed his sword at Jaxon.

This story made me think of my 2019 court cases, when everything that was against me was turned around in my favour. I am forever grateful for my support system, the legal system and the spirit leading me to stand in a position of favour.

Prayer and Prayer Warriors

Here are some snippets from my journals relating to selling the matrimonial house as I worked with the last real estate agent on the final premier house listing to give it the best exposure on the front page of online advertising:

> **Effective Prayer – Ask, Seek, Knock**
>
> "Ask and keep on asking and it will be given to you; seek and keep on seeking and you will find; knock and keep on knocking and the door will be opened to you." (Matthew 7:7 Amplified Bible (AMP))
>
> **Final Exhortations – Encouragement and Prayer**
>
> "4 Rejoice in the Lord always. I will say it again: Rejoice! … 6 Do not be anxious about anything, but in every situation, by prayer and petition, with thanksgiving, present your requests to God." (Philippians 4:4-6 NIV)
>
> **My Prayer**
>
> Lord, I lay my plan to you and pray that your hand is on me and in tune with your spirit. Reveal to me your will and let your will not mine be done for I am nothing and have nothing without you.
>
> The enemy is the same. Breaking us down is how he takes us down, instilling fear and discouraging me from fighting, but I remember Deuteronomy 31 with you, God of Israel, saying, *I go before you. I am with you. Don't be afraid. Don't be discouraged.* You tell me that I am a

> fighter, and so I should stand firm in the trial. I decide not the enemy, so I fight with thanks and praise. You say, *I'll fight with you, and I will fight for you, for this battle is yours. I got you.* As human beings we find security or comfort in other human beings who are fickle when they say this, and so why not find it in someone bigger than us, divine, faithful and never changing? Something new will come out of the crucible, as God says, *I am doing something new, do you not see it? ... I will make a road in the wilderness, water in the desert.* (Isaiah 43:19)

Promise to Self

I had made a promise to myself in the last house campaign. No matter how the next 27 days went, even if no one turned up with the premier listing, I declared, "I believe God is the one who can turn nothing into something."

There was silence for most of that house campaign, then towards the end of it came the two verbal offers I've spoken about earlier from really keen buyers who had seen the house multiple times. Their offers were about $100,000-$150,000 (AUD) less than the initial verbal one received in the very first campaign, over a year before that which at the time, I mistakenly and regrettably did not pursue. (I ended up learning very expensive and painful lessons for life not only with the house sale but the separation. It was all good self-development training). But these offers that were now much lower were like music to my ears after the loud silence. If finalised, they were good enough to pay off the mortgage, realtors, other expenses and even be left with something to move on. Even though the offers were not what we had initially expected, it was good news. God was at work, so in the waiting period I sent out a request to some prayer warriors in the hope of launching a spiritual army.

Prayer Request

This is what I wrote to my prayer warriors from my support network:

> You all know I have had challenges with selling the house and it's been an up and down journey or a cycle for me. I have learned and keep learning in the process. I have had the most traffic this Saturday than any other inspections, which in the past sometimes had zero people turning up (even after paying for the most expensive premier listing advertising to expose the house and doing all sorts of things to put the house in the best light possible). The maths has not made sense, and I have had moments of great confusion, but ultimately, I believe God is doing something great in the spiritual realm for the work has already started in my learning to praise him for 'who he is' not just 'what he does'.
>
> This is the last week of the 30-day premier listing, and I miraculously got the most traffic, with largely positive feedback. There has been talk of getting promising offers from this. This time, I need it to convert to an actual written contract with physical offers and not end up with just talk from buyers. I have come to the realisation that it's a spiritual battle that requires putting on the armour of God and taking a stand (Ephesians 6). I require a spiritual army to stand with me today and that is why I am making a prayer request for you to break bread *with* me and *for* me now.

The Response

From the prayer request, I got a group of people who prayed for me and with me. They were part of the army of angels I had with me here on Earth to fight the spiritual battle I faced. My family is dispersed all over the globe, so they organised a WhatsApp prayer session to share what they each had from their prayer times for me.

My family in the UK, US, Australia and even Zimbabwe, despite its many challenges, made a group call to pray with me, believing in the Word as the guide. There were several readings from different books and insights shared, including:

> "In the same way, the Spirit helps us in our weakness. We do not know what we ought to pray for, but the Spirit himself intercedes for us through wordless groans. 27 And he who searches our hearts knows the mind of the Spirit, because the Spirit intercedes for God's people in accordance with the will of God. 28 And we know that in all things God works for the good of those who love him, who have been called according to his purpose." (Romans 8:26-28 NIV)

> "When Moses' hands grew tired, they took a stone and put it under him and he sat on it. Aaron and Hur held his hands up–one on one side, one on the other–so that his hands remained steady till sunset." (Exodus 17:12 NIV)

> "7 Ask, and it will be given to you; seek and you will find; knock, and the door will be opened to you. 8 For everyone who asks receives, the one who seeks finds, and to the one who knocks the door will be opened. 9 Which of you, if your son asks him for bread, will give him a stone? 10 Or if he asks for a fish, will give him a snake? 11 If you, then, though you are evil, know how to give good gifts to your children, how much more will your Father in heaven give good gifts to those who ask him!" (Matthew 7:7-11 NIV)

God puts people in and around you and there is also a spiritual army that is much bigger fighting for you. The Lord promises victory and even when you feel you can't pray, someone is praying for you.

Know Your Promise

No matter what, be it the ongoing sale of the house, any new upcoming court case or other grey areas, I believed that I had seen the hand of the Lord in my life. I remembered one of the promises I got earlier before all the court rulings in my favour, when all appeared to be going south. It was from the book of Isaiah 61 The Year of the Lord's Favour.

> "The Spirit of the Sovereign Lord is on me, because the Lord has anointed me to proclaim good news to the poor ... broken-hearted ... captives ... to proclaim the year of the Lord's favor ... comfort all who mourn ... to bestow on them a crown of beauty instead of ashes, the oil of joy instead of mourning, and a garment of praise instead of a spirit of despair. They will be called oaks of righteousness, a planting of the Lord for the display of his splendor. They will rebuild the ancient ruins ..." (Isaiah 61 NIV)

It almost seemed like a cruel joke in that moment when I got it. But seeing its physical manifestation boosted my confidence for what was to come.

I recalled at the start of my journey when I was so depressed, I felt so dark and certain that I had been buried for death. I then realised I was buried as a seed to grow not only for my benefit, but for the restoration of others. As clear as day I saw that was my promise and calling, *to be there for others*. When Mordecai and all the Jews were saved in the book of Esther 9:28, they were called to remember and observe those days for generations. Mordecai became second in rank to King Xerxes. He worked for the good of his people and spoke up for the welfare of all the Jews. (Esther 10:3) This substantiated my earlier promise that with the favour in my life I would share the news and serve others in their lives for the good of generations to come as a remembrance of what had happened.

There is much in the world around us that gives us reason to be troubled. Uncertainty and things that are out of our control can even make us afraid, but we are told to take heart. Trust is *active reliance and confidence in God*, not just a feeling. It's putting our hearts, minds and actions in the direction that He would lead us. In a Netflix series I watched, *Sweet Magnolias*, there were two friends facing different challenges (basically, when it rains it pours!) One of the friends posed a question, "Do the storms ever stop?" The other answered, "No, but neither do the rainbows." This is why we are encouraged to stand strong, despite everything else.

In a Disney+ movie, *Rise*, based on the true story of three young brothers born in Greece to Nigerian parents who had immigrated there seeking a better life, there is a scene that beautifully displays how you can find confidence in yourself and what is promised for you. When one of the brothers,

CONFIDENCE & PATIENCE

Giannis, goes to the United States (accompanied by another brother) to see if he can make it in the National Basketball Association (NBA), before meeting Nike, he wonders how he will convince them to be his sponsor. "Why would they choose me over a famous player from one of the big colleges?" he asks his brother. "How do I sell myself against those big names?" He was sure he wasn't who Nike was looking for.

I'm pretty sure at this stage he felt under-confident and that he was *less than others*. His brother says, "Tell them who you are". So, when Nike asks him in the interview what differentiates him from the other candidates, Giannis talks about their journey and how he and his brother would share shoes on court because they couldn't afford a separate pair each. How he slept in the gym to make up time and be able to play the game. How their parents were forced to leave a child behind in Nigeria when they left to form a brighter future for the family. He describes how their family grew up for years running from the police in Greece, the country they were born in, because they were considered illegal. They were forced to grow up as outsiders looking in. He wraps up his family story and the answer to the interview question with: "We work harder. We run farther. We are hungrier because we know the meaning of sacrifice. God has been watching over us, and God will reunite our family again. I just have to play my part."

Confidence is depicted well in Giannis's story and struggle. In the end, the brothers made it to the NBA. When the movie was released in 2022, the three brothers Giannis, Thanasis and Kostas were a force in the NBA. The first two won a championship with the Milwaukee Bucks in 2021 and the youngest with Los Angeles Lakers in 2020.

> "But he said to me, 'My grace is sufficient for you, for my power is made perfect in weakness ...'" (2 Corinthians 12:9 NIV)

Giannis may have seemed a weaker interview candidate, but God's power was made perfect in that weakness, as Giannis was given grace and favour.

In Steve Furtick's teaching,[18] he says that confidence in God's promise without commitment to his process is not dependence but delusion. Being confident that his promise will be fulfilled no doubt involves patience, that spiritual endurance of hanging on despite your greatest trials or sufferings. And you have got to know what your promise is.

What God promised came to me at the start of 2019 in every word written in Isaiah 61 – The Year of the Lord's Favour (as I mentioned above) and at the end of 2019, in Psalms 91 – The Lord my Refuge and my Dwelling. I was consistently reminded of his promise, including on the day I wrote this (12 August 2022) in my five-year-old's morning reading – Luke 4 and Psalm 31 – and in different ways by different people who had no idea that was my promise or that I was going through a specific challenge at the time. It was like God's way of reminding me of his faithful promises even when nothing seemed to make sense.

"It is for freedom that Christ has set us free, stand firm, then, and do not let yourselves be burdened again by a yoke of slavery." (Galatians 5:1 NIV)

At times I've been enslaved by fear, confusion, discouragement and a darkness that steals my confidence and patience in him. I stand fully convinced today he is Lord of Heaven and Earth (even the devil is fully convinced about this more than we even know). The Bible repeats time and again "Do not be afraid ...","Be strong and courageous ...".[19]

To make it we've got to have confidence and courage in someone, something much greater than us to hang on to, and for me that is the Father, Son and Holy Spirit that was left for those who choose to believe in him.

Takeaways

- Accept help from your support system – love from God and those around you gives you confidence.

- Do lots of reading – be it inspirational, self-help or other – and journal your journey.

- Don't see setbacks as failures – instead, take them as lessons learned.

- If you can't change your circumstances, change yourself.

- Know what you have been promised and have confidence in someone or something much greater than you.

COURAGE

COURAGE is not the absence of fear but action in the presence of fear.

Joyce Meyer – Writer and Preacher

Let your love, conviction (of who he says he is) be greater than your fear.

Steffany Gretzinger – Singer

COURAGE's enemy is fear of failure, doubt …

REMEMBER – "She was unstoppable, not because she did not have failures or doubts, but because she continued on despite them."

Beau Taplin – Writer

THE *Mess* HAS THE *Message*

COURAGE – embrace the unknown, unfamiliar.

"Don't follow the path. Go where there is no path and begin the trail. When you start a new trail equipped with courage, strength and conviction, the only thing that can stop you is you!"

Ruby Bridges – Civil rights activist

Instagram Photographer - bartezzz82

The best way out is always through.

Robert Frost

Instagram Photographer - bartezzz82

Take Action in the Face of Fear

As the poet and playwright Robert Frost said, "The best way out is always through". With courage, the common denominator is having to go through and face your fears, doubts or challenges to action or do what it is you need to do.

My fear of getting to my deathbed and facing all the ghosts of what I had in my heart to do but didn't because of fear of failure is what fuels me to take a step towards my goals. The politician and motivational speaker Les Brown put it in other words that hit home:

> "The graveyard is the richest place on earth, because it is here that you will find all the hopes and dreams that were never fulfilled, the books that were never written, the songs that were never sung, the inventions that were never shared, the cures that were never discovered, all because someone was too afraid."

Robert Frost's life was ridden with grief and loss. His father died when he was only ten years old. His mother, wife, daughter and himself all suffered from depression. He wrote poetry at some point in his life to deal with his depression and to take life by the throat, as he said in his own words. He has a short poem, 'Dust of Snow', which resonated with me.

'Dust of Snow' by Robert Frost (1923)[20]

The way a crow
Shook down on me
The dust of snow
From a hemlock tree

Has given my heart
A change of mood
And saved some part
Of a day I had rued

There is hope in the idea that no matter how dark things get, the sight of nature (or a Bible reading or a visit from a friend) can bring about a change in your spirit and help you to utilise a part of your day/your life to take action (no matter if some of it is already wasted).

Despite all Robert went through, he became the most famous poet of his time with multiple awards, and to date, his work is still read worldwide. Even if we might not be at the stage of doing something award-winning, at whatever stage we are, we can work on ourselves to fight our fears or challenges and just do it because it is useful first and foremost for ourselves, and then so we can share with others. Let's not take our unique life lessons to the graveyard.

In Joyce Meyer's confidence teachings,[21] Secret 6 is on taking action. Joyce Meyer encourages us that God works in us through our step of faith, not fear. Decide to be the person he intended with his help.

> "14 What good is it, my brothers and sisters, if someone claims to have faith but has no deeds? Can such faith save him? 15 Suppose a brother or sister is without clothes and daily food. 16 If one of you says to them, 'Go in peace; keep warm and well fed,' but does nothing about their physical needs, what good is it?" (James 2:14-16 NIV)

As in the quote from the book of James above, faith by itself means nothing if it is not accompanied by action; the same goes for courage.

Even though I had problems, my problems certainly didn't have me. I just had to go through the dark tunnel I was in and come out the other end using the spiritual lessons and affirmations revealed to me as I walked through it.

Some of my friends later confessed that with the way I kept standing tall, despite everything that seemed to come at me, they were afraid that one day I was just going to have a breakdown. There is one book I started reading in this period called *Lioness Arising* by Lisa Bevere.[22] Some jokingly said they didn't think I had to read it as the lioness had arisen in me already. Whatever it is they saw in me, I boldly declared that the Holy Spirit that resurrected Jesus Christ from the dead was the same one that was now at work in me, and it said *Peace. Be Still.*

Even when I felt I was getting knocked down I would eventually find the strength to get up and keep on going. When I was in that spiritual space with Jesus, I literally saw myself depicted in the song "Ain't no Grave"[23]: "There ain't no grave gonna hold my body down" and "If you walked out of the grave, I'm walking too …".

> ♫ **To listen to the song:**
> https://www.youtube.com/watch?v=nGncW_ueyHA

I certainly did not see a breakdown on the horizon (though I did spend some dark days in bed with the covers over my head) and could not relate to their concern then. I am glad to say thank God even years after this there have been no breakdowns. It was mostly the confidence I found combined with patience that brought on my courage.

There is also the courage I found in focusing on **one day at a time** with my guidance in the Word. In the book of Lamentations, it says,

> "The steadfast love of the Lord never ceases; his mercies never come to an end; they are new every morning; great is your faithfulness." (Lamentations 3:22-23 ESV)

A devotional from Joseph Prince[24] gave the good news of fresh grace from Jesus to rescue us *every time* we fall short or fail.

Grace is undeserved favour – it is not because of anything we have done but because of who God is. I continuously told myself to stand firm in him no matter the height of the wave in the storm. I truly believe Jesus is sitting right there next to us, just as he did with the disciples in the storm. Don't be like the disciples or the way I was before I knew better. Don't run around screaming, "God! Jesus! where are you?" He is right there with you, always has been and will be. Look at what he does in the storm and follow suit. He keeps his faith, stands up against the storm and gently says "Peace be still".

In the lyrics of the song "Peace Be Still"²⁵ I found the exact words that I intend on continuing to wear whenever fear takes hold of me to remind me to fight with courage: "I'm not gonna fear the storm. You are greater than its roar."

> ♫ **To listen to the song:**
> https://www.youtube.com/watch?v=dUpKZz0Nm7c

One of Nelson Mandela's famous quotes is,

> "I learned that courage was not the absence of fear, but the triumph over it. The brave man is not he who does not feel afraid, but he who conquers that fear."

Our fears should not be what stops us from taking action, but we should have courage to act despite them.

> "… for God gave us a spirit not of fear but of power and love and self-control." (2 Timothy 1:7 ESV)

In the movie *Avatar* there is a good demonstration of courage from Jake, the main character. The Avatar people lost their home and all hope because of Jake's role in their lives. He took sides with the human beings from his land whilst he pretended to be with the Avatar (Na'vi) people as he learned their ways. He stood exposed to those who had welcomed him into their home and culture as an outcast, betrayer, alien, and he felt that to face them again he had to up himself to a whole new level.

To win back the Avatar people's trust, give them hope and humbly plead for his spot in the clan as one of their warriors, Jake had to show them his courage.

Toruk was the Goliath of sky dragons. Nothing attacked him, so he had no need to look up. He was feared and known as 'the Last Shadow' since his shadow was what most people saw. Jake took the courage to face Toruk, bond with him and tame him. When he flew back into the Na'vi's broken home to ask for forgiveness on the Last Shadow's back, they trembled with fear and respect. They accepted his pledge to serve them only and welcomed him to fight the battle with them against the humans.

However, Jake knew he could not do this without help. He prayed to Eywa (the deity of the Na'vi) before the war. He pointed out that he knew he was chosen by Eywa and so he would stand and fight but needed a little (divine, supernatural) help to defeat the other human beings attacking the Na'vi. When his girlfriend, Neytiri, overheard the prayer, she pointed out that Eywa did not take sides but only looked to protect the balance of life.

War broke out, and all hope was again lost for the Avatar people, who were close to being wiped out. But suddenly, the tables turned, and their enemies started falling back with the unexpected help of more Avatar animals. Neytiri called out to Jake in a triumphant voice, telling him that Eywa had heard him.

As I watched the movie, the way the story unfolded reminded me of my reading that morning from the book of Psalms,

> "3 When I am afraid, I put my trust in you, In God whose word I praise ... 9 Then my enemies will turn back in the day when I call. This I know, that God is for me." (Psalm 56:3, 9 ESV)

In turn, this made me think of something I had read about running in the direction of your fears because that's where God is. There was a lion analogy to illustrate this. When lions are old, they have weak teeth and can't hunt and attack. They guard the pride, roar and scare approaching prey so that they run away from the direction of the weak lion to the other side of the pack that has the strong, powerful, young lions that attack without wasting time roaring. It was a good reminder to run in the direction of your fear (running away from a threat will only make things worse) – take courage to stand your ground and fight the fear out in order to live.

With all the challenges and fears that arose with my divorce, I had to learn to face them by changing who I was from within, submitting to God, his voice, believing in the power of the spirit in me and continuing to trust in him. I had to trust him to release his power over my situation as I stood my ground to the end, knowing that just like Jake, who believed Eywa had chosen him for a reason, God has me in this world for a purpose.

Amongst God's many promises to me, there is Psalm 46:

"1 **God is our refuge and strength,**
　an ever-present help in trouble. [my emphasis]
2 Therefore we will not fear, though the earth give way
　and the mountains fall into the heart of the sea …

"5 God is within her, she will not fall;
　God will help her at break of day …"

"8 Come and see what the LORD has done,
　the desolations he has brought on the earth.
9 He makes wars cease
　to the ends of the earth …"

(Psalms 46:1-9 NIV)

My own losses cannot be compared to the *Avatar* movie where many homes and lives were destroyed, or, say, to real-life tragedies like the September 11 losses. Nevertheless, the common ground for me is that the tears are the same colour. The loss, pain felt and the courage needed to live yet another day of life's new normal, when all is said and done, are the same.

What the promise gave me is not that I would not have bad experiences, but that even though I faced tragedy, God was my refuge, strength and very present help in my time of trouble and need. Though it felt like I was in the middle of a war zone, He would not let me fall but help me.

This message was articulated well by Reverend Derrick Harkins in his sermon on 12 September 2011,[26] which he says was inspired by the fact that the family of Army Major Malcolm Patterson, whose life was lost at the pentagon on 11 September 2001, was present. Harkins referred to Psalm 46 and how in that God does not promise the absence of tragedy but his presence in it. His presence is what we can always depend and count on.

The difficult times will come, which does not mean that God has failed us. He promises to be our refuge and present help in times of need. The reverend quoted from a WW2 poem by a Jewish prisoner in the concentration camp, Auschwitz:

"I believe in the sun
even when it is not shining
And I believe in love,
even when there's no one there.
And I believe in God,
even when he is silent.

I believe through any trial,
there is always a way
But sometimes in this suffering
and hopeless despair
My heart cries for shelter,
to know someone's there
But a voice rises within me, saying hold on
my child, I'll give you strength,
I'll give you hope. Just stay a little while …"

Have Faith in the Plan

> "In their hearts humans plan their course, but the Lord establishes their steps." (Proverbs 16:9 NIV)

The reason fear holds us back most of the time is because we see the mess attached to it and not the message, but if we change our mentality to see that the mess has the message for our good, ultimately, we will take courage despite the bad. In one of pastor Joel Osteen's[27] sermons, he talks about an expected end and how God will turn your mess into a message. This is a lesson I learned firsthand in my journey and can attest to. In Jeremiah 29:11, God says his plans are for good not evil to give you a future and hope.

Understanding that your expected end has already been established should give you the courage to soldier through the scary and not so good to get to the good. It is ultimately good news. Your end is not in defeat or failure but in success, victory and fulfilling your purpose for which you were uniquely set apart in this world.

Joel Osteen gives us a movie analogy; like any good movie there will be twists and turns in our lives. This happens even when you know you are headed in the right direction and meant to be going this way, but you find yourself going the opposite direction. You question yourself: my goal is that way, so why am I headed the wrong way? There will be scenes that don't make sense – divorce, sickness, setbacks in different areas, be it your finances or whatever else.

What you don't realise is that this is not your final scene. If you are breathing, your movie is still going. Remind yourself that this is not how your story ends. You have an expected end from the Creator of the Universe, God Most High, who has planned your future for good, not harm. If you keep moving forward, at some point, you will come to another twist, but this might be a good break, a promotion, healing and so on. God knows how to weave it all together.

You see this principle in the life of Joseph. God destined him to become a great leader, to rule and help the Israelites during a time of famine. His end had already been established. Joseph started off well. He was his father's favourite and went around wearing a colourful coat from him that represented favour. At seventeen, his life had an unusual twist; his brothers were jealous and sold him into slavery.

Joseph had a dream he talked about where he was shown he would rule a nation. He didn't get discouraged. He knew that his end had been planned, so he kept going and doing his best. He found favour with his master and was made head of the household, then was falsely accused by the master's wife. He was thrown in prison, another unusual twist that made it seem like he was moving away from his destiny after doing what was right and refusing to engage with the master's wife's sexual advances. The real test of life is, will you stay in faith when doing the right thing, but the wrong thing is happening? Will you be at your best even when you are not getting the credit for doing what is right or good? Will you have the courage to keep going despite the challenges? This is where Joseph excelled.

In the Waiting

I had been a sole occupant of the house for almost a year when a new Family Court application was raised due to my failure to sell, and this time, it felt rightfully so. By then I had tried all the different strategies and advice for a successful sale. I had nothing to offer and was ready to surrender, as I had thrown everything I had at it. I could understand this court case too, since, with us living separately, the expectation was that the house would be easier to sell. At this stage, my latest realtor had gone above and beyond applying all sorts of suggestions, tips and tricks to get the house to sell; it just hadn't happened yet. Getting a written offer from the previous year was still a work in progress. The market had gone through changes and uncertain times, too. It was initially the Australian election impact and then the Covid-19 talk starting to emerge. It was just all getting amplified.

Being the human I am, when I got the verbal offers from the two keen buyers in December 2019, a part of me imagined celebrating Christmas with a contract in hand as I rejoiced. I got an update from the realtor that one of the very keen buyers pulled out, and I was at peace with the news, as at this stage, I had come to understand there is news of this world versus the truth of the word of God in the Bible. I had to keep the faith, even though, despite the prayer request and building of the spiritual army, instead of getting a written contract, there was a withdrawal.

I journalled at the time: 'I stand now able to differentiate this as news versus God's truth who says with man it's impossible but with God all things are possible. I choose to stick with God, his truth and keep digging deeper into the Word – seeking and praising him. I am at peace, no darkness now and even if it comes again, I choose to remember the truth: it's the shadow of his wings. As he did for David saving him from Saul, he does that for me now'.

I noted the common themes I got that week were on considering the trials to be pure joy and that his grace is sufficient.

> ♫ **To listen to a song on the theme, follow the link to 'Your Grace is Enough' by Chris Tomlin:**
> https://www.youtube.com/watch?v=vpYtYYaTFGQ

From December to the New Year holidays, I didn't hear back from the other keen buyers as they went away for that period, and I continued to wait. The main message I felt repeated in my spirit and that I wrote down was that *God is in control*. A family member sent me a phone message saying, "I was listening to this yesterday and it jumped out at me for you". It was titled, "God has got this". This message came after I had asked God if I was on the right track and to get someone to confirm to me in an ABC kind of manner. It was a jump-up-and-down exhilarating response!

When I faced obstacles, my part was to be strong, courageous and know that with him in control, I would overcome because he overcame death. It meant that, **Obstacles bigger than me = Opportunities for God to show who he is.** Overcoming the mountain is like fuel for when you are faced with the next one. He did it then, and he can do it again.[28]

> ♫ **To listen to the song, 'Do It Again', which inspired me:**
> https://www.youtube.com/watch?v=ZOBIPb-6PTc

As mentioned, I had re-signed with my agent for yet another campaign to sell the house in 2020 as he advised that whilst waiting for a written contract from the keen buyers of the previous year, we had to keep going.

From the very start of the campaign the traffic was amazing, almost as if people were falling over each other to see the house and see who could grab it first. I truly felt that God was at work. There were even repeat viewers: the husband was keen and wanted a house in that new estate. Both husband and wife admitted to liking the house, said that it was priced well, but his wife had issues with construction on one side of the house and the

COURAGE

upcoming one whenever that would happen on the empty block on the other side. There was absolutely nothing I could do about my neighbours' construction as it was all within reason in a new estate. The potential sale fell through. I was devastated.

I wrote down in my journal, 'I think this part of this chapter of my life is called *In the Waiting*'. I felt like Joseph as I knew there was promise of good, but I had to stand in courage despite the bleakness of the situation. I was running out of cash, and my finances were on shaky ground. I could possibly face repossession of the house by the bank if I failed to keep up with repayments. I was waiting for God, the other buyers, the right buyers and the right time for it all. I had to keep at it with the inspections, plus choose to remain courageous and hopeful.

Previously, I felt so dark and had such a heavy spirit that it took me days or weeks to shake off the rejection when buyers' responses didn't turn into a sale after the light of hope that they were the ones. This time around, even as I scraped the bottom of the barrel with my finances, I was at peace with it all and chose to trust that God really was in control. Even when it seemed dark, I chose to believe that it was the shadow of his wings, and no matter what, I stuck with the truth of His word over my life despite the news and reports of the world. I understood that wherever I eventually landed, even if it was with nothing or more debt, that would be the right spot, and I had to pick myself up from there.

I shared my story with one of the real estate agents who in turn opened up about her previous similar challenges and how she got to build her own real estate agency. She had owned a house, got married and then ended up losing it all to her now ex-husband and his girlfriend. At this point it was years down the track and all that was in the past, but it was that 'mishap' that had driven her to create the real estate agency she now owned in our area. She made the choice to keep going from where she landed, even though she was left with absolutely nothing. It didn't mean the pill wouldn't be a bitter one to swallow, but I found it enlightening. I had no idea how I would do it if that ended up being my case with my sole parental provision and other responsibilities to meet as well, but somehow, I had to find the courage to keep going.

I got even more perspective from the book of Acts 27:1-44. Paul was travelling to Rome, Italy and had been a prisoner for two years as authorities didn't know what to do with him. He had said that he wanted to plead his case to Caesar. He was then intending on preaching from Rome to everywhere else. On their way there, there was a storm, yet Paul knew that was his destiny from God. At some point, all hope was lost, and it looked like they were going to die. It was dark and they had to throw cargo overboard. In the chaos, Paul stood with the courage he had from God's guidance and told them not to be afraid, they wouldn't die, only the ship would be wrecked.

I heard a Sunday service teaching that said that the humble confidence in God that Paul had in this story is what the world needs. Paul said, "take heart" and "have faith in God". In life, the ship that you protect and put your trust in instead of God might have to be wrecked for you to eventually get back on course.

When amid the storm people wanted to jump off the ship, Paul said the only way to be saved was to have courage and stand their ground in faith by staying on that same ship. He broke bread and gave thanks to God in the middle of the storm – this is definitely encouragement for us to do the same in our storms!

All were saved after the shipwreck and a plan for the soldiers to kill the prisoners didn't go ahead because of the centurion who wanted Paul saved. Take note how special favour in your life can also save others like you or around you. Not only was Paul saved, but the other prisoners too. In my storm I chose to break bread, give thanks not only on my own but also prayed with family and friends. I knew by being courageous I stood to see the favour upon my life not only for my good but for others, too, in whatever shape or form that would be.

In *Harvest Moon*, a movie I watched on Netflix, the daughter thanks her dad, saying that courage even in the tough times is the most valuable gift you can give your child. She had learned that it was even more valuable than a trust fund from him. This, I believe, is the lesson I had to learn in the delay and challenges I had experienced since the separation and divorce. Had everything worked out as swiftly as originally planned that would have saved a lot of heartache and money, but I would have lost all the other invaluable lessons learned and not ended up in exactly the place I was meant to be for my good and that of others.

"Fear not, for I am with you; be not dismayed, for I am your God; I will strengthen you, I will help you, I will uphold you with my righteous right hand." (Isaiah 41:10 ESV)

I was still scared of the feelings of rejection, but then again, I was reminded that my desire for success had to be greater than my fear of failure. My greatest fear was to be like the Israelites who went back into the desert for forty years after standing on the verge of their breakthrough, all because they were too scared to face the final battle with the people who stood between them and their promised land of milk and honey. They were afraid to face the giants with trust and faith in the Lord. My fear was also stopping at day 6 when on day 7, the walls of Jericho that had stopped me from accessing my breakthrough would all fall. With all my fears I chose to face the giants, though my day 7 in real life took months rather than days to come to fruition.

Our Response

My greatest fears are:

- being complacent, staying and/getting back into the old pattern of things or accepting that as my best

- accepting what those around me or society want me to accept as the norm, yet I know there is more for me and won't fully realise who God is, my dreams or what he has in store for me

- ending up on my death bed with "what ifs" as my legacy.

It's how I respond to these fears that will be the game changer.

With all that we go through and choose to fight against all odds, we stand as a light for our families, friends, colleagues, others like us and so on because of that courage. We have our different ways of dealing with and pressing on through all that happens to us internally and externally. For me, hanging on to the word and name of God was part of the biggest reason I pulled through.

In the song 'Tremble', sung by Amanda Cook, there is an interlude where she speaks about how it's not about how loud we yell his name but about the authority in his name and the whisper of his voice over your life. There is a light placed inside of us, and it's just that we are not reaching for the light to turn it on. We must look at our response in fear and question ourselves whether we choose to turn on the light, act in courage or leave it off, stay in darkness and live in fear.

As the song goes, Jesus's name is a light that makes darkness tremble and silences fear. The song calls my bones (that I thought were dead to be buried) to live, and my lungs to sing and praise his name (so that I can be a light for others).

> ♫ **To listen to the song, including the interlude:**
> https://www.youtube.com/watch?v=jo-fcUmIO2E

I am telling you my story in the hope you will find the courage to keep going too. Find a way to tap into your spirit and switch that light on. Sometimes the process is painful and hard, BUT don't forget when God is silent, he is doing something great for you!

COURAGE

Takeaways

- Take action in the face of fear so you'll have no regrets about things you didn't do.

- Focus on one day at a time.

- Don't expect the absence of dark times but see them as an education.

- Ensure your desire for success is greater than your fear of failure.

- Never give up.

PART 3

Through the Recovery, Self-Discovery, Battles and Victory to the End

FORGIVE

FORGIVENESS is love in action – it's a process, a journey – about you letting go, doing good despite the bad

Colossians 3:12-14   New International Version

12 Therefore, as God's chosen people, holy and dearly loved, clothe yourselves with compassion, kindness, humility, gentleness and patience. **13** Bear with each other and forgive one another if any of you has a grievance against someone. Forgive as the Lord forgave you. **14** And over all these virtues put on love, which binds them all together in perfect unity.

THE *Mess* HAS THE *Message*

Bear with each other and forgive one another if any of you has a grievance against someone. Forgive as the Lord forgave you.

Colossians 3:13

Instagram Photographer - bartezzz82

Forgiveness is a process and form of love that you need to apply as you let go of the bad and do good instead. At times it might be about forgiving yourself or others for whatever it is you feel is pulling you back. Forgiveness is for yourself and so **choose to love yourself by letting go**.

Take Responsibility

Forgive Yourself

My strength, reminder and counsel come from reading the message in the Word and Jesus's teaching. In the case of losing my mother – when I initially got the news from my older brother that something had happened to her, I remember breaking down and crying. She was involved in a car accident where her car was hit by a truck that tried to overtake on a bend, hitting the car my mum was in and causing it to lose control. She was coming from work out of town with three other colleagues. The driver and other passenger at the front didn't make it. My mother and another passenger survived to make it to hospital. My mother was the last survivor. She lived for three weeks post the accident and when she passed away just before Christmas, it had appeared she was on the mend.

With the accident and her death, it's as if I was numb to a lot of things. I was there – but not really there – for the funeral. I recall cuddling up and comforting my sister – who had come from the UK at the later stages – when she cried, being there for my dad when everyone else had left to go back to life as usual, as my younger brothers found their own way of dealing with the grief by going away for sleepovers with our relatives.

My feelings were kind of absent from that whole process for the longest time, and it only finally hit me years later. I was a teenager when my mum passed away. I cannot remember my last goodbye to her, but I do recall every now and then we would have fights. My mum loved hugs and the last I remember is her wanting one and my not reciprocating. She then made a comment about how I loved my dad, and I didn't respond that I loved her too even though I wasn't happy with her about whatever we were fighting about. Having that fight as one of our last memories did sting when I lost her forever because I don't know how she would have felt in that moment, and I wanted her to at least have gone knowing that I loved her.

In time, I have learned to let that go for myself, and I make sure I let my family know I love them. As for the driver of the truck, who survived, I just had no feelings.

It was as I mourned the death of my marriage that I eventually did grieve my mother. It was in this period that I finally managed to leave that past behind and take only the lessons learned plus the goodness from having known my mother in the time that I did. Her passion for the word of God, putting it into action in her life for herself and the good of others, helped me to pick up on that for myself, too.

When it comes to my ex, in our union as boyfriend and girlfriend through to us getting married, I played a part in what happened between us. It takes two to tango. Even in the separation and divorce. From the beginning of our relationship, I did know that we had similarities that made our union stronger and differences that had the potential to undermine it, and even though I might not have fully understood how they would impact us, I went ahead with the relationship anyway.

With the breaking down of the relationship I also later came to a fuller realisation and understanding of my part. How my shutting down in silence would have impacted my husband. With the new depth of clarity I gained, I began to feel deeply sorry for that. I caused a world of hurt for him, too, and damage to our relationship. His choices and how they affected our relationship are separate from my accepting my individual weaknesses. I had my own contribution to own that I was aware of and needed to also do the work to let go, to forgive myself for my faults and work on a better version of myself.

Years later I came across a podcast along similar lines of how it takes two to tango by Travis Barton and Tiffany Ann Beverlin from Dreams Recycled[29] – inspirational stories that mainly focus on divorcees. Tiffany talks about how divorce is kind of seen as the stepchild of adversities, with people tending to blame someone else for it, although after a little while those people find themselves faced or stuck in the same situation.

When we face adversities, whether relationship problems, job loss, financial or health situations, it is all about how you deal with it. In those difficult situations, life in general seems to be doom and gloom. The more we wallow in it, the more comfortable depression can feel. Tiffany didn't get out of bed for eight months. Travis admits that it can be comforting to blame someone else, but part of the change process involves us taking some responsibility, no matter how terrible the other person or situation.

We are encouraged to shift that powerlessness and blame mindset to help us avoid being in bed for months or stuck in the negative. We need to start taking responsibility instead and move to being powerful. With this mind shift, we transition to a positive position of being able to do something about it. Ask yourself, *how can I become better as a result of what happened? What lessons did I learn from my experience that I can now apply?*

In the movie, *Little Black Book*, there is a scene where Stacy, the main character, comes to a similar realisation.

Stacy: How does a girl who falls; no, actually jumps eyes wide open, down a rabbit hole, plummeting into chaos come out unchanged?

Stacy: She doesn't.

Joyce: A clean break is easier. You can reset it, and it heals, and you move on, but if you leave things messy, and things don't get put right, then it just hurts, forever.

Stacy: I was ready to try again, a little bruised, a little humbled and hopefully, a little smarter. I believe we write our own stories and each time we think we know the end … we don't.

Stacy: Perhaps luck exists somewhere between the world of planning, the world of chance, and the peace that comes from knowing that you just can't know it all.

Stacy: You know, life's funny that way. Once you let go of the wheel, you might end up right where you belong.

Stacy learned that adversity inevitably leads to change, and ultimately, our destination. With all the chaos in my life that had occurred, and that I participated in creating, I, like Stacy, realised in my brokenness there was no coming out unchanged. In the conversation above, Joyce highlights that if we don't deal with the ensuing mess, then we will carry the hurt associated with it forever. Essentially, we'll be stuck in a loop.

Even though Stacy admits to not knowing it all, she is ready to try again after all the changes. She also realises letting go will get you to where you are meant to be. I, too, do not know it all but choose to trust in God and his guidance for that. I also choose to work on getting to where I belong by letting go and letting God as he encourages us to forgive. As you forgive yourself or learn to forgive yourself, you must do the same for others and learn to forgive them as well.

Forgive Others

Keep aiming to do good despite the bad. Chris Williams was hit by a drunk teenage driver, Cameron, in a car accident on 9 February 2007.[30] The accident killed his pregnant wife who was expecting their fifth child, his second eldest son and his only daughter. His eldest son was with friends and his youngest son survived the car accident. It was an out-of-body experience for Chris as he wailed in grief and realised that he had lost his family. Spiritually, emotionally and physically he felt crushed.

Friends of Chris visited him and his surviving son in hospital, and they said that one of Chris's first questions was checking in to see how the young man driving the other car was doing.

Chris says that for the first few months after the tragedy, he was in shock over the huge part of his life that was lost. He found it difficult to kneel and have a conversation with the Father in Heaven when he was in such anguish and feeling so lonely. When he did, he felt that it was an interesting first conversation because God didn't immediately try to make it all better; He just listened to him.

When he had this deep sense of loneliness and anger, Chris didn't direct it at the drunk teen driver but towards the Saviour. He found that getting the anger off his chest was helpful, and at the end of each of these conversations with God, he felt that he had ultimately learned something about God the Father's son, Jesus.

Chris still had not come to terms or comprehended how the accident had happened, but he did sense that he needed to let it go. His friend says he felt there was the Jesus way to resolve the problems, address and handle the sorrow, and there were also other ways, but he felt Chris had already clued in on which way to go earlier on in life.

When Cameron, the teen driver, eventually met Chris for the first time, he said that Chris wore a smile that he couldn't reciprocate as he knew that he was facing the man whose life he had ruined. Chris willingly talked about what had happened that night, how he felt, and he didn't mince his words as he said all Cameron needed to hear.

He also told Cameron that he should let go of what had happened and encouraged him to pick a date to move on. After witnessing Chris's attitude in this situation, the teen driver felt grateful and strengthened.

When Chris sat down with Cameron, he said that his forgiveness was merely the power of the Saviour at work through him. Referring to the hope in God is what helped Chris address and end episodes of grief in his life. His burden was made light with forgiveness, and in turn, that same forgiveness was a pure demonstration of love in action for what appeared unforgivable.

There is also forgiveness even when a person doesn't know or acknowledge they are wrong. I had a chat with a friend on the topic one day. They were struggling with someone who had wronged them, and I told them how funnily enough I had tuned into a Brisbane radio station the day before with a similar topic on 96.5 FM – the DJs posed a scenario whereby someone had decided to forgive, and the other person made a comment about how they had not done anything wrong and didn't need forgiveness. There were a few responses that came through regarding how to process that reaction. Ones that hit home for me were on how forgiveness is about *you*.

> *Forgiveness is not about the other person but about you releasing (letting go) and so the other person's response is irrelevant!*
>
> *The other person should not be a factor – whether they realise it or not.*
>
> *Staying angry or keeping the hurt of the person who hurt you is like drinking poison and hoping they die.*

It's only when that drinking poison analogy was used that the actual picture of unforgiveness fully came to life for me. I thought it was the funniest and silliest thing to do, but as human beings we do it. **Unforgiveness is something you hold onto to kill yourself.**

A few days after, I literally saw the words – 'Forgive someone who isn't sorry' – on the wall of a Brisbane shop on James Street. I took some photos for my friends as proof, just in case they thought I was making it up. God does talk to us all the time if we put ourselves in a position to listen. At times someone might not be sorry at all as they do not see their wrong, they might say sorry without sincerity or what might not seem sincere to us, but either way the end goal is the same: forgive for your own good.

A grandmother of one of my daughter's best friends at day care also shared her wisdom on how she advised her other grandchild who was then in primary school and facing bullies. She was a little chubby and had a few encounters with some mean kids at school about her weight. She had told grownups about it. Her grandma said that instead of wearing a bad attitude when they called her names, she needed to serve them a good attitude by wearing a smile and saying, "Thank you for letting me know", then walking away with her head held high. When her granddaughter did that one day, her response left the bullies dumbfounded as they expected a negative reaction. I loved it and it brought further clarification to my reading about overcoming evil with good.

In various versions of the book of Romans 12:14-21, sometimes called Love in Action (NIV) or Forgiveness (Berean Standard Bible (BSB)), we find the following:

> "Bless those who persecute you …"

"... don't avenge yourselves for it is written: "Vengeance is Mine; I will repay, says the Lord."

On the contrary: "If your enemies are hungry, feed them; if they are thirsty, give them something to drink; for by doing this you will heap burning coals of shame on their heads. Don't let evil conquer you, but conquer evil by doing good." (Romans 12-20-21 NLT)

"Do not repay evil with evil or insult with insult. On the contrary, repay evil with blessing, because to this you were called ..." (1 Peter 3:9 NIV)

"... love your enemies and pray for those who persecute you ..." (Matthew 5:44 NIV)

From my mess at the peak of my separation, pending divorce conflict and hurt, I needed help on how to overcome evil with good, so I continued meditating on forgiveness and pondering different people's take on it whenever I came across the topic.

I read this line from *Conversations with God*[31] – "I have sent you nothing but angels, everyone who enters your life – little, small, or big, good, or **bad** [my emphasis] – is a fellow angel there to teach you something."

Before I came across this reading, I had not fully considered the 'bad'. It helped me recognise that I needed to view those people who were bringing hurt and pain into my life as nothing but angels. Not so easy to do! This certainly felt like a sick joke.

I had no energy or idea how to pray so I tuned into a TV church service and the reading that came up as I did was from Isaiah 43:

"I am about to do something new; even now it is coming. Do you not see it? Indeed, I will make a way in the wilderness and streams in the desert." (43:19 BSB)

It seemed the joke was getting worse and all I could manage to say in that moment was, "Well, God what are these fellow 'angels' teaching me now –

what is the something new that I do not see yet, that you promise will be like a road in the wilderness and water in the desert?

The Word and my Father's promise of something that seemed almost impossible kept me digging, kept me on a positive tangent, despite the mess in my life that seemed to escalate.

In the book of Matthew, when teaching about Love for Enemies, Jesus says:

> "... love your enemies! Pray for those who persecute you! 45 In that way, you will be acting as true children of your Father in heaven. For he gives his sunlight to both the evil and the good, and he sends rain on the just and the unjust alike. 46 If you love only those who love you, what reward is there for that? Even corrupt tax collectors do that much. 47 If you are kind only to your friends how are you different from anyone else?" (Matthew 5:44-47 NLT)

Regarding vengeance this should not be our concern. Some say that karma deals with it, as what goes around comes back around. In my case, I believe it is the Lord's to do as he sees fit.

My part is to do good to all the fellow angels he sends my way, especially the bad ones. Forgiveness is indeed a process. At times, when I thought I was doing well, I would be challenged with something worse to force me to go deeper into myself.

I follow some practical steps to reach forgiveness, which I will share with you below.

The Benefits of Forgiveness

The theme of forgiving to be successful came to me via a story about Tyler Perry,[32] the actor and filmmaker. Tyler Perry says his big success in acting only came when he had forgiven his dad, who was physically abusive to him and his mother growing up. When he understood his dad, who he was and what he had been through and not what he had done to him as a father – he decided to forgive.

Some say when negativity or the past calls, call on your superpower because the past can't be altered, and your future doesn't deserve the punishment. We are encouraged to overcome daily and not let the negative or past kill us.

There was a church service I attended once that referred to the story in the book of Luke 4, where Jesus returns to his hometown of Nazareth and is rejected. After Jesus talked, the people tried to kill him, and it is said that he walked through the crowd and went on his way to the next place and continued with his work. You need to make this choice to move on and walk through the negative or it will destroy the work you are trying to do.

At another church service, a pastor's wife told the story of how she worked with a woman who rubbed everyone the wrong way. She found her intolerable and talked with her husband about how badly the woman behaved. He replied that sometimes when you have a difficult person or circumstances that you must deal with in your life, *you* must change rather than expect the other person or the circumstances to change. If you don't change, you might find yourself having to deal with either the same difficult person or another difficult person or circumstance again and again. Look at what you must give in your spirit, find what you have to learn from it and change. With my journey, I realised I had to work on my not-so-good behaviour – such as the way I shut down, how I speak to others, and that I have to check in on my feelings and listen to others. Overall, I have learned and still am learning self-awareness to see how best to use my strengths and rein in my weaknesses.

Steven Furtick put it another way. In the book of Psalms (Psalm 55) when David asks for wings like a dove to escape from his troubles, what we must realise is that our troubles come from within. Even if you escape into a new job, place, relationship or whatever, if you have the same troubles deep within you, then you'll pretty much take them with you and won't really be escaping. For many of us, our pasts are littered with painful memories and experiences we would rather just forget. But for some reason, we can't. Our past hangs over our heads like a dark cloud, stealing our joy and hope from today. But this is not the life that Jesus has called us to live. We are encouraged that, no matter what has happened in our past, Jesus has called us to a greater future in him. I aim to live a full life, and at some stage, I realised without forgiveness I end up living in the past and so limiting not only my success in life, but my freedom, hope, joy and happiness.

We have been forgiven so many times by God, and so we are called to forgive others too. The Bible talks about praying for your enemies and blessing them. How to do this with sincerity is to pray for them in the same way you pray for yourself and want to be blessed or understood when you seek God for your own wrongdoing. It is hard to hold on to grudges when you pray for them like that. We need to remember to love those who persecute us and love others as we love ourselves. Empathy, often described as the highest form of knowledge, then comes into play. Certain acts could take years to fully forgive, but empathy is most certainly a first step in the right direction on the forgiveness journey.

From the book of Ephesians 6, I learned that it helps with the forgiveness process to understand that it's not an actual person per se we have challenges with, but the evil spirit at work within them that is essentially using their body as a vessel. The word says it's not flesh and blood that we are struggling with, but powers of this dark world, spiritual forces of evil in the heavenly realms. Bearing in mind what we are up against, I realised that I didn't have what it takes physically to keep standing and overcome the challenges I had with people in my life. I have had to consider the greater forces at work within them. It was necessary to find ways to forgive the physical person and fight against the spiritual forces at work with the power of the Holy Spirit that defeated death through Jesus Christ.

Reading the same book, I was encouraged to put on the armour of God to fight, which is rooted in the word of God, the truth. In Jesus's name I stand changed and am changing still. I have learned and keep learning to forgive to set myself free. I let go and let God be the judge as I release the bad in my life. To do that, I need to make changes to the way I think. *As you think, so you become.*

"For as he thinks in his heart, so *is* he." (Proverbs 23:7 NKJV)

"Do not be conformed to this world but be transformed by the renewal of your mind." (Romans 12:2 ESV)

Forgiveness Is a Process

Through my therapy sessions and other readings, I learned a process to reach forgiveness. When seeking forgiveness, we can find a scripture or a positive thought that relates to that situation somehow. Write it down or meditate on it throughout the day or each time you have the negative thought. If there are any lingering feelings, then redo the process. It is a process that can be repeated, and your heart will soften as you go through it until, eventually, you let it go. Work on this with the end goal of overcoming evil with good. Without the process, you will repeatedly accumulate negative feelings whenever you are wronged. The positive thought or scripture reminds you to say that this is the truth about the circumstance even though what's happening around you or your feelings might tell you otherwise and want you to veer off from the positive or truth.

Every time we are offended, it can create negative energy. We could choose to use the energy towards forgiveness or doing something good instead of rallying and tallying with other people about the wrong done to garner support from them. We need to take it to the Lord in prayer.

It may seem strange, but the best time to forgive is before the offence ever happens, so learn to prepare your heart by choosing to forgive in advance and protect your peace. This is not to say that you are rallying for an offence but preparing yourself for the future as you ready your heart and mentality to release the negative before it happens. For example, you know that with summer coming, there is a possibility of an anthill in your driveway – choose to prepare how to deal with it instead of kicking up a fuss about it when it comes. Pastor Joel Osteen explained it well in his teaching on protecting your peace[33] – stop falling into the trap of getting upset by the same things in those situations where people know how to push the right buttons to steal your peace. Decide ahead of time to protect your peace in adversity so you can tap into that power and remain calm.

Joel Osteen tells the story of a man and his friend who went to buy a newspaper. There was a very unfriendly clerk. The man bought his paper from the grumpy person, who acted like he was bothering him, then said to him, "I hope you have a great day!" The clerk didn't even look up. The man got no acknowledgement of having said anything. His friend asked what was wrong with the clerk and if he was always that grumpy, to which his friend replied, "Yes". His friend then asked if he was always that friendly to the clerk, and the response was affirmative. When he asked him, "Why?", the man replied, "I made a decision not to let another person ruin my day." Basically, he had packed his spare tyre so that if he hit a pothole, he could just get on with it. He would not stay back and be rude, arguing with someone who had upset him.

There are people you might deal with who have a gift for getting on your nerves. It's like they are poisoned, and they exude poison. Don't let their bad attitude get to you. The good news is that you are in control. They can't make you unhappy unless you allow them to. When a certain situation or person upsets you, there is an issue that they are not dealing with. Decide well ahead of time to find a way to respond with love even when rubbed the wrong way. Choose to be kind and respectful to those who are unkind or disrespectful to you and don't let their poison contaminate you. With an offence you at times feel the person has taken away your choice to be joyful, peaceful and not be offended, though the reality is, they haven't. You have the choice, the power to put love in action and overcome.

Steps to Forgiveness

There are some practical steps to forgiveness that I came across and implemented in my journey too. At times, forgiveness is a one-off. Other times a deeper engagement is needed, which requires more work from within and with God. With my marriage struggles, I chose to separate for each of us to work on our issues as individuals and aim to become a better version of ourselves, firstly for our own good, then for our beautiful baby girl, as our relationship had become toxic. The environment was not conducive to caring for oneself as an individual or each other, let alone another little human being who was fully dependent.

I had decided to forgive by the time we were officially separated. I told myself that even if hurtful things were done, I would aim and choose to do good. This was not seen as such from the beginning, and some said I had not forgiven because of my decision to separate. I genuinely didn't get where these people were coming from as in my heart of hearts and in what I chose to do, despite everything, that is not what I felt or intended.

By the time we officially divorced after a year of being separated under the same roof a lot more had happened, and I still stood by my decision to forgive. I stopped trying to justify myself and resorted to saying maybe forgiveness is like peeling an onion and I just hadn't gotten to a certain layer that people saw or wanted me to be at. I didn't fully know what I meant by it all, but I later found some Proverbs 31 Ministries[34] lessons that helped enlighten me and bring it all full circle:

- **The decision to forgive is a one-time event, but the process of forgiveness is a progression.** The fact that there are two parts to this was indeed like a light bulb moment for me. There was certainly the one-time event in the decision to forgive, and there was also the progression or process involved with the forgiveness. This differentiation in the decision and the progression or process is the one that I failed to articulate or that others tended to miss, misunderstand or not acknowledge. This could be the layers of the onion I was referring to. I felt I could relate to this and kept working on it.

- **Learn how to apply practical steps to a situation in your life today and let go of unforgiveness.**

- **Compassion and empathy for someone who wronged you are necessary to find grounds for forgiveness.**

When we make a decision *not* to forgive, it doesn't just affect us. There will be a far-reaching impact, even if we don't realise it. Consider the hatred Joseph's brothers felt towards him in the book of Genesis. This had a sort of domino effect leading to the chain of events that resulted in Israel's oppression in the book of Exodus.

How do we forgive? Sometimes the process of forgiveness is lost in the command of forgiveness. It is more encouraging when we consider it takes practice, and it is a process.

When someone does something to you that's deeply hurtful, painful, offending or wounding, some steps to consider are:

1. IT'S HEALTHY TO WRITE DOWN FEELINGS

a) Jot down all the feelings you are having or that situation created – not just what you are feeling in the moment like 'I am angry, lost, sad'.

b) List/tap into previous wounds/deep hurts. Write them down. If someone says something to you, and it deeply hurts you, it may be a trigger, tied to the fact that you already wonder whether what they say about you is true and could be an indication of an insecurity you already have or verbalized.

I wrote down my feelings during the turbulent separation/divorce period. Some of what I felt was:

- mostly sad, alone; misunderstood; betrayed; like I was dying – dark; afraid; angry at times; broken into pieces; abandoned; lost

- ashamed (initially but not anymore), confused (like I was caught in a whirlwind), doubted myself, betrayed, angry, hurt; very sad, in mourning; shattered – not into pieces but beyond recognition; buried for death (only later I realised it was buried for growth)

- suffocated; trapped; frustrated; tricked (only now I am more alert); betrayed.

I realised when some labelled me stubborn, it could have triggered my fears from the past, and it was probably the best of me playing bad. For it to play well, I had to find a way to use that quality for good as a relentless fighter instead.

2. HAND THE FEELINGS OVER

The handover allows us not to park our feelings but acknowledge that they are real and there. If we don't do this (handover process), it can create buildups that lead to explosions! My choice was to hand the feelings over to God by *physically writing them* down per the suggestion from Proverbs

31 Ministries. You have the option of finding an equivalent way of handing over your feelings.

- Take all the feelings you have written down.

- Fold over the paper – if you choose to physically write them as encouraged – and address them to God to help you deal with those feelings in a healthier way.

It is important to actively hand the feelings over, so you have a marked moment.

I choose to journal and hand mine over to God to help me by memorising a verse or verses relevant to my feelings and bringing them into the areas I'm wrestling with in prayer or fasting. For example, with my feelings of anger, I recite even to date James 1 (NIV):

> "... be quick to listen, slow to speak and slow to become angry, 20 because human anger does not produce the righteousness that God desires. 21 Therefore, get rid of all moral filth and the evil that is so prevalent and humbly accept the word planted in you, which can save you.
>
> 22 Do not merely listen to the word, and so deceive yourselves. Do what it says." (James 1:19-22 NIV)

When I find myself angry, it helps as a good reminder to bring me back to what I need to do – be quick to listen, slow to talk and get angry. Without that, I find I keep struggling. I am not perfect through all this, but I have taken some steps in the right direction. God, who I choose to hand over to and be my guide, "is gracious and compassionate, slow to anger and rich in love." (Psalms 145:8 NIV)

3. COMPASSION, EMPATHY – WRITE DOWN ANY HURT THE OTHER PERSON COULD HAVE GONE THROUGH

I realised that someone's own experience is what could lead them to do what they do to you.

We might not know what has hurt someone, but to feel compassion, we can imagine that what they said or did to you is what a loved one said or did to them. Without compassion, it is difficult to get to authentic forgiveness.

In trying to forgive, I tuned in to the person that hurt me, putting myself in their shoes to write down some feelings associated with their encounters from a young age to adulthood:

- abandoned
- unhappy, sad; betrayed
- betrayal by God, others; hurt
- given up on Christ, stone cold to never feel the hurt again
- abandoned again; rejected

I realised how what was happening in the present could have triggered those feelings of abandonment, betrayal, rejection and their actions may have been a way to try to regain some sort of control, be it consciously or unconsciously, done in a good or bad way to protect themselves.

Knowing and considering some of the hardships they would have encountered at a young age definitely built up compassion and helped me empathise, even though I knew as adults we have choices to seek change and be a better version of ourselves.

4. WRITE OUT A TRUE STATEMENT OF FORGIVENESS FOR THIS PERSON

Writing it down instead of just saying it will engage our brain to actually understand what it is we are forgiving a person for and accept it fully. By doing this you are also marking a moment of forgiveness – you can say I've already marked off forgiveness for that hurt and aim to move on without pulling previous hurts into the new hurts should there be more offences. This is similar to the practice that Chris encouraged Cameron from the car accident to apply by picking a date to let go and move on. I imagine the fact that he handed over such advice to the person who killed his family meant he had applied that process to get himself there, and it had clearly worked.

I forgave what was done to me in the past, current and future to either hurt me, frustrate or stir me up or put me in a precarious situation. I believe it was done possibly out of feelings of abandonment, betrayal, rejection, and it was a way of protecting themselves from their past experiences and the current situation.

This statement of forgiveness does not mean that when I am triggered I don't get angry or have certain feelings. However, having written it down definitely brings back that compassion and the reasons why they do what they do to help me empathise. In addition, I have some go-to words of wisdom from the memorised verses to help me work through it in a healthier manner.

Triggers & How You Respond

One day as I was driving from the airport, I heard on the Brisbane 96.5 FM radio channel a lady saying something along the lines of – you will have triggers in life, but how you choose to respond to them is 100 per cent your responsibility. Before responding, you need to take the time to examine the inner you, identify why that something is a trigger and avoid acting in the heat of the moment.

When I looked inside myself, I realised my ex's repeated offensive behaviour had become a trigger for me. Possibly my doing as he demanded in a bid to seek peace or prevent escalations enabled him to keep pushing boundaries. He didn't seem to believe he was doing anything wrong, and those around him or close to him appeared to have reached the stage where they didn't have any more to say, so they either remained silent or were his cheerleaders. I kept asking myself, what can I do to avoid the same cycle, especially with the repeat offences?

In the movie *Full Out*, which I mentioned earlier, as the gymnast Ariana Berlin recovered from her accident, she was told she should now be able to walk on her own. But even when your body heals, your mind can still be broken. By this time, I was recovering physically, and I was gaining much-needed weight. However, I still had more work to do on my mind.

Ariana's UCLA Coach, Valorie Kondos Field, said in the film, life is about choices and it's from your decisions you can design your own life. The mother of some of my close friends said to me I had to train myself to reach a point where I didn't act in the heat of the moment based on triggers. Everything we do in life is a choice, and those choices determine what kind of life we are going to live. I eventually came to a realisation that the trigger or repeat offence of another could be foolish behaviour, but my repeat response to that makes me the bigger fool. When you know better you can do better. I had to work on changing how I respond and still am as I progress.

I used the Bible as my compass to help me work on my mind. Jesus's last words on the cross in the book of Luke are "Father, forgive them, for they do not know what they are doing". (Luke 23:34 NIV)

Some more words of wisdom from another encouraged me not to hold onto unforgiveness. Don't wait for the other person to come to you. Be the first to act – don't hold onto pain or bitterness. Don't repay bad with bad; repay evil with good for that is our calling. (1 Peter 3:9)

> "If you forgive those who sin against you, your heavenly Father will forgive you." (Matthew 6:14 NLT)

This is the Lord's prayer:

> "Forgive us our sins, for we also forgive everyone who sins against us. And lead us not into temptation." (Luke 11:4 NIV)

Love forgives – forgiveness starts by forgiving yourself, then extending love, mercy and forgiveness to others, especially those who are your enemies. On the verse of the day Bible app, Nona Jones (preacher, speaker and author) said: the things we don't forgive in other people turn us bitter and in turn we hurt other people. We turn out not to be fun people to be around. We can't be kind and compassionate to others or salt and light to the world when we are filled with bitterness or unforgiveness for others. Be kind, compassionate and forgiving to be a light.

Each day, I choose to keep working on myself to reflect light and not darkness. The sweetest revenge is choosing to live the best of your life without dwelling on those who have hurt you – choose forgiveness, choose love.

Takeaways

- Forgiveness is a process.

- Follow the process to forgive yourself so that you don't wallow in depression.

- Follow the process to forgive others so you don't get caught in a loop and repeat the same negative behaviour.

- Remember that part of forgiveness is forgiving someone who isn't sorry.

- Recognise your triggers to better avoid falling into traps.

LOVE

LOVE is the answer.

Love never fails … now these three remain: faith, hope and love. But the greatest of these is love.

1 Corinthians 13 (NIV)

Love the Lord your God … Love your neighbour as yourself.

Matthew 22

Love your enemies and pray for those who persecute you.

Matthew 5

Love in Action – overcome evil with good.

Romans 12

Love is not just a feeling but an action (a decision)

Levi Lusko (Pastor)

THE *Mess* HAS THE *Message*

What Is Love?

"Love is patient and kind. Love is not jealous or boastful or proud or rude. It does not demand its own way. It is not irritable, and it keeps no record of being wronged. It does not rejoice about injustice but rejoices whenever the truth wins out. Love never gives up, never loses faith, is always hopeful, and endures through every circumstance." (1 Corinthians 13:4-7 NLT)

"But I say, love your enemies! Pray for those who persecute you!" (Matthew 5:44 NLT)

This is a command, and there is a decision to love. Loving people isn't easy, especially when it comes to people you disagree with or who are unkind to you. The question then is, how do you love them? I have been faced with this challenge several times as have most, if not all, of us. My dad said to me that we love through the truth and the Word. The Word says to pray for those who have wronged us. You need to change the way you see them. As discussed under the steps to forgiveness in the previous chapter, empathy must come into play.

Cindy Beall[35] from Life Church says that our demonstration of love may not always be well received, but it also never depends on how the other person responds. We are simply called to love. *Ruby Bridges* is a Disney movie based on the true story of an African-American six-year-old girl's heroic struggle in breaking segregation in New Orleans' public schools in 1960 and the lessons drawn from it. In the film, Ruby's doctor questioned what it was that kept the little girl going in her adversities. He eventually realised it was her family support system and faith in God's teaching. Her resilience came from the love of her family as they reminded her how they loved her and how God loved her, along with the biggest Bible teaching – love.

Love your neighbour and love those who persecute you. Ruby's teacher, Barbara Henry, who was the only one willing to teach her despite their different skin colour, also showed Ruby her heart and hoped the other teachers would follow her example. Doctor Cole had volunteered to help

Ruby, expecting her to be stressed from all the pressure due to the hate surrounding her at school because of her skin colour, but he saw no signs of stress. To be brave and take action despite fear, you need to have something you ground yourself in, a faithful foundation.

The doctor recalled an incident where Ruby stopped and was seen moving her lips. He asked her what it was she said to the crowd. He wondered whether she had finally cracked and was responding in anger. He was taken aback when Ruby explained that she was praying for them. Despite the fact that they were nasty to her, she asked Jesus to forgive them, for they didn't know what they were doing, just as Jesus had prayed to forgive those who treated him despicably.

Through courage and an act of love, a six-year-old managed to break a barrier for other children like her to eventually start going to schools that were previously forbidden due to segregation.

To date, Ruby Bridges[36] still uses lessons from her story to fight racism in schools, saying that it is all to do with love and caring for the other person as a human being. She believes that love is the key and her story is a demonstration that love never fails.

Love comes in different forms. There is the love of God, a higher being – comforting to know that it's from someone you can always trust. You can love yourself, so you have a tank full to also love others as you love yourself. There is also love for and from others – you can love others like you, those who aren't like you and above all, those who have wronged you.

With all my ups and downs, as I chose to root everything in the Bible – one thing that rang the loudest is how it can all be summarised by one common theme – love. Everything from the books in the Old to the New Testament boils down to teaching us about love.

> "36 'Teacher, which is the greatest commandment in the Law?' 37 Jesus replied: 'Love the Lord your God with all your heart and with all your soul and with all your mind.' 38 This is the first and greatest commandment. 39 And the second is like it: 'Love your neighbour as

yourself.' 40 All the Law and the Prophets hang on these two commandments." (Matthew 22 NIV)

How ironic that it took a journey through depression and refusing to pray (though, as I mentioned earlier, I was open for others to pray for me wherever they were) to my relationship falling apart to learn to rebuild myself again using the very thing that was lost – love, the greatest teaching of all. I know this – I am not perfect, not where I want to be, but I am certainly not where I used to be. The word is my guide. Despite our imperfections, we are called to pursue Christ, who is perfect.

With each situation I try to find a way to pause and dig deep to see how to love and put love in action as I've learned that **love is not just a feeling but a decision to act on**.

> "… if I have a faith that can move mountains but do not have love, I am nothing. 3 If I give all I possess to the poor and give over my body to hardship that I may boast, but do not have love, I gain nothing." (1 Corinthians 13:2-3 NIV)

Love Your God

Love for God involves listening and obeying him through his word and prayer. Jesus says, love your enemies, love others. This love is what he did on the cross for us, and the true meaning behind Easter. He welcomed our wrongdoing, our sinful nature into his own perfection by giving up his own life. By accepting his welcome, we are changed. We form a new relationship with God the Father through Jesus's name, the blood he shed for us and the Holy Spirit that resurrected him from the dead and was left for us as our guide as he ascended into Heaven.

Love Your Enemies

Love your enemies in a way that you can, instead of hurting or being angry. This could entail praying for them/doing something good for them.

There is a saying that goes:

If you don't heal what hurt you, you will bleed on people who didn't cut you.

Hurt people hurt people =

everybody who hurts you is simply doing it because they were hurt themselves.

You can cut that cord, stop the hurt, so you don't continue passing it on.

However, it's easy to love those we choose to, but not so easy to love people we encounter in our day-to-day lives, especially without choice. It becomes challenging when we conflict with those who are different from us, wrong us or rub us a certain way, don't like us or share the same values, tastes, backgrounds or ideas.

There is a Netflix movie, *Best of Enemies*, a real-life story that exemplifies doing something good or showing love to those who wrong you and loving others as we love ourselves. The story focuses on the rivalry between an African American civil rights activist, Ann Atwater, and Ku Klux Klan (KKK) leader, C.P. Ellis. Ann Atwater stops some teenage boys from destroying KKK material on display at a desegregation meeting and puts it back in order, saying that they need to read it, not rip it up. She teaches them to see it as the Klan giving them a window to look through, a way to understand them and get the upper hand. As she hangs up a KKK uniform, Ann is visibly shaken. This is all observed by C.P. from afar.

Clearly, loving the enemy and overcoming evil with good is a challenge, a process, and comes down to you choosing to forgive – to put love into action. When Ann later learns of the struggle that C.P. has with his disabled son Larry's care facility, where he must share a room since C.P. can't afford a private one, she can relate, empathises with him and seeks a favour to have Larry moved to his own room. Having his own room makes Larry calmer, and his whole family is also at peace.

Love and empathy are powerful tools in the fight against unforgiveness (in which you are only killing yourself) and on the journey to seeking freedom through the forgiveness process.

> "Love your enemies! Do good to them. Lend to them without expecting to be repaid." (Luke 6:35 NLT)

Love Your Neighbour as Yourself

In the TV series *Queen Sugar*,[37] Nova, a journalist and activist, visits a young boy in jail and encourages him to pray. He says he doesn't anymore. He is in jail for something he didn't do and refuses to say that he is guilty of it. She strengthens him by telling him how the enemies operate – they break you down to get you to accept a plea for something you didn't do, to scare you, they pile a mountain of charges and make you afraid to fight. I found this to be true when we face our own enemy, enemies, or opposition(s) in life, especially as it can be an accumulation of attacks, one on top of the other. Nova tells the boy that he seems like a fighter – take the trial, *you* decide, not them. The boy insists he didn't do anything wrong, and Nova says, "Fight, then I will fight with you." The boy agrees, and she then says, "I got you".

My take on this picture of Nova clearly loving her neighbour as herself was also that the decision to fight and face our challenges – depression, mourning, divorce, sole or single parenting or whatever else – is up to you. With that so-called stubborn streak in me, the best of me playing bad, I decided to channel my relentless fighting spirit to face my demons one at a time.

In the book of Deuteronomy, God of Israel says:

> "Going to War
>
> 1 When you go to war against your enemies and see horses and chariots and an army greater than yours, do not be afraid of them, because the LORD your God, who brought you up out of Egypt, will be with you.
>
> 2 When you are about to go into battle, the priest shall come forward and address the army.

3 He shall say: 'Hear, Israel: Today you are going into battle against your enemies. Do not be fainthearted or afraid; do not panic or be terrified by them.

4 For the LORD your God is the one who goes with you to fight for you against your enemies to give you victory.'" (Deuteronomy 20:1-4 NIV)

As I have faced my battles, I have had the spirit and God's words lead me out time and time again.

Incidentally, I literally had to apply the 'love your neighbour' approach with my own neighbours. They reneged on a promise to pay us their share of the cost of a fence at a later stage as we were the first to build. (My ex supported this neighbour in their stance, adding unnecessary challenges to the sale process.)

With my neighbours' refusal to pay for their half of the cost, it seemed they were throwing the kind gesture of accepting to receive the fence funds at a later stage back in my face. As for my ex's position backing the neighbour, it was just baffling, but I prayed for God to take his step as Father and deal with it all.

I eventually received an email from my neighbour with a receipt of fence payment. The payment coming through despite it all was a bright moment in some dark times.

Love from Those Who Love Us

Love from those who love us, those we trust, is like fuel to keep us going. I found out from my dad after my mother's passing that she knew through one of her visions that her death was near and had prayed for more time because she had young kids. She had thought that she was given three years, but it turned out to be exactly three weeks. My sister also told me how my mother had 'banked prayers' for her husband and all her children. I didn't really know what that meant at the time, but especially in the period when I didn't have my one-on-one relationship with God and did my own thing, I believe it is through my mother's banked prayers for me that I managed to pull through certain events.

As I got over my numbness about her passing when I mourned the death of my marriage, I learned to feel and let go of her death. I used my spiritual eyes to see what was left to take from it. There was an evening tradition my mother had implemented a year before she left us, where we prayed together as a family before bedtime. She would get us to take turns leading the prayer each night and pray for others. She got a map of Africa and would get the leader to pick a country to pray for – a country at war, in dire poverty or whatever. As a child, I certainly didn't enjoy this tradition as it felt forced upon me, but once I came of age, what I learned from it all is the love for others in need that was engraved in not just me but my siblings from this tradition and my mother's banked prayers.

At different points in life, my dad and each of my siblings have become involved in charity work in whichever country we are based as we each feel it is our vision or purpose in life. Part of this for me is through JDE foundation, which I mentioned earlier. This charity aims to love others in need through partnering with existing organisations to support work for children in poverty as well as women in coercive control relationships.

There is also a lot of love fuelled by my mother-daughter moments with my little girl. I had a mighty big thud as I missed a step on my way from my bedroom to go downstairs to my then three-year-old. I fell on my bottom, and it hurt so bad I wailed in pain and forgot I had my child with me. Her concerned little face, the panic as she too started to cry, was the only thing that stopped me. I had to stifle my crying as I looked for a way to mask the pain. Her questions, asked out of love, "Mummy, are you okay? Did you break your bum? … Should I bring you an ice pack?" had me burst into laughter. That and her care with the ice were very soothing. (This is what I do for her when she is in pain.)

A tradition she started with one of her uncles when she was little is when they went for a walk or to the park, she would pick a flower to bring for me. It had been quite a while since she had done this, when after one of the Covid lockdowns, she went to the park with my dad and unexpectedly brought back a purple flower and a very teensy-weensy yellow flower, saying, "I know my mummy loves flowers. I love you. You're the best mummy in the whole world". I was blown away by her big talk and gesture of love. I was also especially amazed how she managed to bring the tiny yellow flower to me in one piece.

When she was about two years old at the peak of my struggles with sole parental care and with a year behind me of doing the lion's share of the work, I was exhausted. As we were driving somewhere, she made a random comment from the back seat – "Thank you, Mummy, for taking care of me. I love you". These little surprises all made it worthwhile, and to say they were like a light in my world or fuel to keep me going would be an understatement.

Love Others

> "Love never fails ... now these three remain: faith, hope and love. But the greatest of these is love." (1 Corinthians 13:8 NIV)

Ultimately, what we are called to do is love others. I read and jotted down the above Bible quote one morning when I hadn't had the greatest of starts with my little girl. My aunty had helped for two months when my daughter was about one and a half years old, just being there for me in any way I needed. Fast forward to about another year and a bit later, my dad had come to live with us to help me with any house responsibilities, the move to the new house and alleviate any other duties he could. That morning, I just did not have it in me to deal with my daughter's demands and drove off leaving her with my dad. I had no idea where I was driving to, but I ended up at some lookout where I decided to do my morning Bible reading. As I did my reading and writing, I realised the name of the restaurant there was LoveWell Project. It caught my attention and triggered me to look up the story behind its existence.

LoveWell Project café was birthed by Hope Foundation to help with changing women's lives after working in the sex industry.[38] It's a story of loving others who are like you or your neighbours as you love yourself. Having been a sex worker due to drug addictions, Bronwen Healy managed to make radical changes to find her way out. The café was a way for her to help other women like her with addictions or in the sex industry who wanted to change their lives by giving them job opportunities as well as raising funds for the charity through the takings.

Our weaknesses are what lead us to the light when we do the work and from there, we can also then be a light for others in the world.

> "If I could speak all the languages of earth and of angels but didn't love others or had not charity, I would only be a noisy gong or a clanging cymbal." (1 Cor 13:1 NLT)

At times we forget to love as we are called to. We might be greatly gifted with languages as per the verse or in whatever else, but without love for others, it's a misuse of our gifts.

Through treating others as important or more important than ourselves, we discover true humanity, just as Jesus did. In *Beauty and the Beast*, the moral of Belle's story is for things to become loveable they must first be loved, otherwise we end up with hurt people who then hurt people.

Albertine is a song and story I heard at a creative conference from Brooke Ligertwood née Fraser, a New Zealand singer-songwriter (this was well before she was a Grammy award winner) that best summarises everything noted in loving others.[39] The song was birthed from her Rwanda visit. As a volunteer there she felt inadequate, thinking less of herself amongst doctors, nurses and other people with practical skills. She was a singer-songwriter and didn't know what she could do to help. When she met Albertine, she was humbled as she listened to her genocide story. She knew she had a responsibility to see through: she had to write a song about Albertine and Rwanda. The song became a hit and reached millions who now felt they also had to do something about the genocide there.

It was by listening and *thinking of herself less* and more of Albertine and others that Brooke managed to see how her skill was in fact useful to bring about awareness on a world platform and call for others to help. She brought hope for Albertine and others like her in Rwanda, and she encouraged others in the world to also act as she sings in her song "faith without deeds is dead" (inspired by James 2:14-26). Ultimately, she wrote a song driven by love. Brooke listened to Albertine, loved her as she would have wanted to be loved and put her faith into action as the greatest of all love.

> ♫ **To listen to the song:**
> https://www.youtube.com/watch?v=BXApy0IegKs

I believe that by using whatever gifts we have, God will match things up so that everything works out together for good. If we get out of our heads a lot more, we will come to realise that we each have our own unique place in this world, just like a piece of the puzzle. Our story and gifts are part of this jigsaw puzzle, and it all fits together. Perhaps you have no idea what your gift is. I have come to realise it might not even be about your ability but your availability to be there and just do what needs to be done; then the rest will fall into place.

With the separation there was a stage I felt so ashamed, embarrassed of everything, myself, our conflict, especially how public it went (with my family and friends) and the breakdown of the marriage. I wore shame and vulnerability until I realised that journalling to tell my story brought about illumination for my healing process as I worked on starting to piece myself back together again.

Coincidentally, by blessing, one of my friends had a creative conference ticket they couldn't make and gave it to me. It turned out to have been the best timing in every way. I was no longer holed up in the house at that time as I dug my way out of depression. Joined by another group of friends for the trip, I packed my less than one year old daughter and my bags to head to Sydney for it. One of the things that was of interest to me was the storytelling/writing as at that stage of my season – difficult/challenging as it was, I felt I wanted to share my story so that others didn't walk in my shoes. I learned about creating art for others through your own story and allowing them to feel understood and share theirs. It was at this creative conference that Brooke shared her story on Albertine and the song that she created out of it.

Create art in whatever form your gift leads you and not only will you be saved and freed, but others will also find the same saving grace and freedom.

Redemptive Power of the Love of God

At a church service, a man named Dan shared how when his kids argue amongst themselves and when one won't help with something, he empowers the other with, "Dad says so" to get things done. He then had a conversation with God – why not apply that to himself when facing challenges? (Why not say to himself, "God the Father says so"?)

> 6 For to set the mind on flesh is death, but to set it on the spirit is Life and Peace … 11 if the spirit of him who raised Jesus from the dead dwells in you, he who raised Christ Jesus from the dead will also give life to your mortal bodies through his Spirit who dwells in you." (Romans 8:6, 11 ESV)

Attention to God puts us in a spacious place; as a child of God, we are more empowered, giving us greater freedom.

Focusing on yourself means your eyes are off God. Realise not *who* you are, but *whose* you are, his child = "My Dad says so", the one who defeated death.

At a church service, Sheila Walsh[40] shared that when her mum married her dad, she wore some beautiful pearls. Sheila lost her dad, a man of faith, to a brain aneurysm at thirty-four years old that transformed him into an angry man who seemed to hate her. Now her mother's beautiful pearls, and how they came to be, have become symbolic for her – a sand grain goes into an oyster and irritates it. Because of the irritation, the oyster coats and recoats that grain of sand with saliva and calcium. At times, it can take up to three years to form a perfect pearl.

Sheila relates this to a story she heard about Kendra Graham's eight-year-old who had dyslexia.[41] It was taking her over an hour to do some homework that really should have taken her about ten minutes. When her daughter threw her pencil at the wall, her mother heard her frustration and offered to help, but the little girl responded saying that it was okay, she was just busy *making some pearls*. (She had watched a sea life movie the previous night). She equated her homework struggles with the way an oyster forms a pearl – out of the irritations in our life something beautiful can be formed.

For Sheila Walsh, who struggled with depression in early 2020 to the extent that she had difficulty getting out of bed some days, the eight-year-old's story was a gentle reminder for her to think of the gift of pearls in the tough times. When her husband checked in to see how she was doing, she, too, responded with, "I am busy making pearls!" Remember, when you struggle with the challenges in your life – health, financial, relationships, whatever – that something beautiful can emerge from all these struggles.

Sheila's mother coated her own irritations in life with grace and love, and Sheila drew strength from that. Our Father in Heaven's love is based not on what you get right but on who he is. God doesn't look at any of his children and say, "I love this one better"; he just loves us all.

When Sheila's mother died, she was meant to get her engagement ring, but it got lost and she received a picture frame that said, "Yes, Lord" instead, which she found more valuable. She used to laugh at her mum and say, "Mum you don't even know what it is you are saying yes to!" Her mother would reply, "But I know *to whom* I am saying Yes – God of grace and love."

By saying "yes" to God, I am reminded that I am loving him, which is the first and greatest commandment.

> "Who shall separate us from the love of Christ? Shall trouble or hardship or persecution or famine or nakedness or danger or sword? 36 As it is written: 'For your sake we face death all day long; we are considered as sheep to be slaughtered.' 37 No, in all these things we are more than conquerors through him who loved us. 38 For I am convinced that neither death nor life, neither angels nor demons, neither the present nor the future, nor any powers ... will be able to separate us from the love of God that is in Christ Jesus our Lord." (Romans 8:35-39 NIV)

Even in all my suffering when I was so broken, I found his saving grace, his love threaded throughout my story at every point, even when it didn't seem like it at times. He weaved something beautiful with it all, making me realise the mess in my life has the message. There is a Japanese art called *kintsugi* – golden joinery or *kintsukuroi* – golden repair. It is artwork to repair a piece of broken pottery by filling the cracks with gold to make something beautiful. The breakage and repair work are treated as part of the beauty of that pottery. Embrace your history, the life changes, flaws or imperfections to make something new, better and stronger, just as the Japanese art teaches us. There is no attempt to hide the damage, but it is in fact illuminated by the repair. You are more beautiful for having been broken.

In the movie *Love Struck Café*, Megan's late mother had a quote she hung in the café: 'Don't tell people your dreams – show them'. Megan says her mother may have died too young, but she got to live her dream. She envies that because she feels her dream is right in front of her for the taking yet just out of reach! Megan's friend responds that our dreams are hard to reach and that's what makes them worth reaching out for.

This reminds me of the Maltesers chocolate in our vending machine at work. There were about two or so packs just hanging by a corner out of the rack, ready for the taking, yet no one could get to them. It was all so close and yet so far, as they say.

In the film, Megan faces a conundrum with her property development project potentially failing and losing her job if the house preventing the project progression can't be sold. Her ex challenges her, saying that in life, we blindside ourselves and look at a problem as having two options, but what if there is a third option? Megan questions what that is, to which her ex says he doesn't know, but he has found that by admitting that there could be another solution, one ends up showing.

What I admit to as my solution that ends up showing even when I have failed is that time and time again God is love and that what he calls us to do is to love him first – listen and obey him. I have found it is just as it is written in the Word, and it all ends up working itself out as all things work out together for good for those who love God. I choose to admit God has the other option, so all I need to do is obey or follow him.

In the end, when Megan talks to the house owner again (who was adamant that she wouldn't sell), she says to Megan that if she can put her heart into it and come up with a plan that respects the beauty of the place they live in (essentially for her neighbours), then she will consider a sale. Megan does eventually come up with a plan to build a profitable development that will respect the environment and entices the house owner to finally agree to sell.

Learn and keep on going just as a baby does. I watched our baby girl when she learned to walk. She would fall and giggle away with her cute little laugh, then pick herself up again and walk two or three more steps. The progression seemed super slow. In a week she could finally walk a whole corridor. Before that it was almost a whole year of prep from tummy-time sessions to sitting up, commando crawling, crawling, walking holding onto things, clumsy standing, then a few steps walking and plenty of falls on repeat for about a week to this full-on clumsy corridor walk. It was amazing to watch it all as it happened right in front of me. It left an imprint on my heart – a reminder that no matter how many falls I have, I should keep on going and love God. I choose to trust in his grace in my weaknesses and just say, "Yes, Lord", like Sheila Walsh's mum.

Even If You Keep Falling – Love

> "I am convinced that nothing can ever separate us from God's love. Neither death nor life, neither angels nor demons, neither our fears for today nor our worries about tomorrow — not even the powers of hell can separate us from God's love." (Romans 8:38 NLT)

You might feel like that pain and anxiety from your challenges or being mistreated is part of who you are. Kneel in a position of surrender and come before the Lord. Jesus is the greatest weapon, the perfect love that casts out all fear and disappointment.

> "Whoever lives in love lives in God, and God in them." (1 John 4:16 NIV)

My conviction as to who God the Father is, and my belief his teaching all comes down to love, only fully sank in with my trials when I formed a one-on-one relationship with Christ and read the Bible on my own to connect with the Spirit. Remember his love, grace and mercies never end and are new every morning, so even if you have learned a lot and continue to try but keep falling, keep trying and try again – and give thanks and praise to keep you going.

TAKEAWAYS

- Use empathy to love even those who are unkind to you. Do something good for them or pray for them to avoid hurting. Remember, hurt people hurt.

- Use the love from those who love you to give you strength and fuel to keep going.

- Embrace your flaws or imperfections, use your life challenges to make something new, better and stronger.

- Spread the love and share your story, so that others don't walk in your shoes.

- Remember you are beautiful for having been broken.

THANKS & PRAISE

THANKS and PRAISE is how you fight your battles.

Thanks and Praise

– even in the not-so-good times, play the Glad Game
– for the 'what' not the 'why'
– what you learn in it all; for what you have despite the not so good
– for 'who' he is. He is love through it all.

"Tell God what you need and thank him for all he has done. Then you will experience God's peace, which exceeds anything we can understand. His peace will guard your hearts and minds as you live in Christ Jesus."

(Philippians 4:6-7 NLT)

Instagram Photographer - bartezzz82

"Whatever is right, whatever is pure, whatever is lovely, whatever is admirable— if anything is excellent and praiseworthy— think about such things."

(Philippians 4:8 NIV)

Instagram Photographer - bartezzz82

> "You can't go back and change the beginning, but you can start where you are and change the ending."
>
> *C.S Lewis*

Time and time again, in adversity, challenges or loss, one of the greatest tools I have found to fight my battles has been thanks and praise. These affirmations are the foundation for the other ten in this book. Giving thanks and praise to help start our day enables us to keep going on a positive tangent, whether in the good or bad times and provide a lifeline during the challenging days. I have found that faithfully applying these affirmations throughout the day, as I would with medication, has helped maintain my well-being and given me the power to go on.

Power in Life's Challenges

Even with our marriage breakdown, I wanted my daughter to know of her wonderful capacity for love. My prayer has always been that our family story will be a light for us and others not only from lessons learned but in also striving to become better versions of ourselves, for our good and for others too. I give thanks not for the death of my mother, my depression or marriage breakdown, but for all the good that came out of the challenges faced. I praise God for who he is. Some say challenges *in life* could be God's way of getting our attention, and I can say that I found this to be true in my case. When I did eventually choose to seek him in my own time as I crawled out of my fog of depression, I saw how he walked me through each challenge, ultimately pointing out the message in my mess.

In the story I recounted earlier of Chris Williams who lost half his family in an accident,[42] when Chris reconciled with Cameron, the teen drunk driver, he did eventually realise that he was grateful for the tragedies and trials. Gratitude not because any of it was easy or desired but because our challenges help us love. As a man acquainted with grief and sorrow, he got to learn his purpose in life. He rebuilt hope in his in-depth relationship with God and realisation that he was not facing the challenges alone. Whatever love and strength he showed, he was simply mirroring that from his understanding of that relationship.

From Cameron's end, he and his family were overcome by thankfulness for Chris's strength in how he acted towards them in the situation. Cameron's mother said it felt like all the despair was washed out when he freely forgave her son.

Some say it is not about how you start but how you finish. From being a stay-at-home mum who was told she was unemployable and had no skills, Tiffany Ann Beverlin from Dreams Recycled eventually managed to pick herself up amid the pain from her divorce. She couldn't have imagined herself as the woman in tech, CEO, bestselling author and podcaster that she is now. Life and business coach Travis Burton[43] says when we are at our lowest, we have the most potential to become our greatest because of the emotional leverage to do it. We should pick up the pieces and put ourselves back together again and become even more extraordinary than we ever thought possible.

As far as anything drags you down, it raises you up, and you can use it for good. Tiffany believes engaging in her passions came from her adversities, which were like a reset button. Physically engaging in your interests, be it setting up a podcast, website, journalling, writing, photography – whatever it is that needs doing, even if you must learn it, can help with figuring out what lights you up, especially if you don't know what your passion is. Instead of wallowing in the relationship lost, Tiffany looked at all the other opportunities. Now she is involved in working on something she loves and is grateful for it. Your choice and response to your adversities is what defines you. We are presented with two choices: to change or redo the same thing repeatedly – choose wisely.

> "20 Now all glory to God, who is able, through his mighty power at work within us, to accomplish infinitely more than we might ask or think." (Ephesians 3:20 NLT)

In a church service, Linda shared how she now feels she is operating in a place of peace and love from depression after her son Tim had an accident and needed his parents' permanent full-time home care. She encourages strength in speaking the word of God. Keep repeating scripture to yourself over your life until it comes to life. Linda repeated the Word from Psalm 43:

> "5 Why am I so sad? Why am I so troubled? I will put my hope in God, and once again I will praise him, my saviour, and my God." (Psalms 43:5 GNT)

At times I found that thanks and praise came out of a place of weakness to give me strength. One of my staple thanks and praise prayer songs at the height of my trials was a song that came to me from my sister on a day she checked in on me. I had been back at work for a little while with home life still mostly upside down. I was forced to move out of our home with my daughter who was eighteen months old at the time in order to accommodate the arrival of my aunty as my ex didn't want her at our home. She was coming to help me with the baby care and house maintenance duties to present it for sale. We had to temporarily live with some friends and hoped that would bring some peace with my ex.

At the time, my little girl was still drinking a lot of milk and eating yoghurt for solids, which meant sleep intervals were every two hours on a good night. On a not-so-good night, she would be up every hour or so. In that phase, I would literally watch the sunrise and couldn't fall back to sleep with the erratic sleeping pattern, so I would get myself ready for work and then, when her time was up, get her ready for day care, which was now another half hour or so farther than our usual place of residence. I generally wasn't feeling particularly fresh, with little to no sleep.

One day, on top of the copious challenges I was facing, I somehow managed to drop my new laptop out of my bag as I sat by the bus stop. It got dented in one of the corners and the screen had numerous cracks. I simply felt like it was just one thing after the other, even with the smallest things, and I completely lost it. Forgetting that I was in a public area, I broke down sobbing and didn't care if anyone saw me or my ugliest of cries. I was having a terrible day and I wanted to permanently get out of the rubble of trials and challenges I was under, but it seemed I couldn't budge. My glimmer of hope and a spirit change (a bit like the spirit change Robert Frost experiences in the poem I mentioned earlier) came later in the day from a conversation I had with my sister as she comforted me and then sent me a song – 'Surrounded (Fight My Battles)'.[44]

> ♫ **To listen to the song:**
> https://youtu.be/vx6mfAgHDsY

As I played it and sang along, something shifted, and I felt that with all the trouble I was in, everything was also okay. To date, when I play this song, my spirit finds peace. It is like some say: when we praise God, he doesn't change, but we change.

Giving thanks and praise is also a giving to ourselves as it transforms our spirit. If you need peace, love, wisdom, patience, then begin to praise God of peace, love wisdom, patience and he will transform you to be like him. I was interested in the story behind the song, and I learned the songwriters were inspired by the book of Chronicles where King Jehoshaphat faced a vast army against him.[45]

The Moabites and Ammonites with some of the Meunites came to wage war against Jehoshaphat, and the king cried out to the Lord, "Our God, will you not judge them? For we have no power to face this vast army that is attacking us. We do not know what to do, but our eyes are on you." The Lord responded saying, "Take up your positions; stand firm and see the deliverance the Lord will give you, Judah and Jerusalem. Do not be afraid; do not be discouraged. Go out to face them tomorrow, and the Lord will be with you." The king then appointed men to sing to the Lord and to praise him for the splendour of his holiness as they went out at the head of the army, saying: "Give thanks to the Lord, for his love endures forever." (2 Chronicles 20 NIV)

"As they began to sing and praise, the LORD set ambushes against the men of Ammon and Moab and Mount Seir who were invading Judah, and they were defeated. The Ammonites and Moabites rose up against the men from Mount Seir to destroy and annihilate them. After they finished slaughtering the men from Seir, they helped to destroy one another. When the men of Judah came to the place that overlooks the desert and looked toward the vast army, they saw only dead bodies lying on the ground; no one had escaped." (2 Chronicles 20:22-23 NIV)

Taking their position, standing firm, then singing praise and thanks to the Lord is how they won. From it came the aha moment for the songwriters that thanks and praise is how we fight our battles.

The other inspiration was from a reading in 2 Kings when Elisha and his servant were surrounded by armies. With his servant standing in fear and hopelessness, Elisha prayed that the Lord would open his eyes to see that those who were with them against the armies were far greater than those who surrounded them.

For me, it was clear as day in all that, that though it might look like I am surrounded by enemies, I am in fact surrounded by the Lord and his goodness. When there is darkness, it is the shadow of his wings (as it says in Psalm 57 (NIV), "I will take refuge in the shadow of your wings until the disaster has passed"). For the spirit of heaviness, we are encouraged in Isaiah 61 to put on a "garment of praise".

From the story of King Jehoshaphat, we see how he and his people stuck strong in their resolve as they stood firm in the word of the Lord, though they seemed not to have a chance in the world.

There is another story that strikes a similar chord that I later heard from Eddie Pinero (Motivational Speaker and Podcaster from Your World Within).[46] In ancient Greece, King Leonidas led a small army that was a fraction of the size of the vast army led by King Xerxes of the great Persian empire. Before the invasion of Greece, the Persian king implored their king to surrender their weapons and got a response from Leonidas saying "Molon labe", meaning "Come and take them". Despite all odds stacked against his small army, Leonidas stood firm, showing a superpower type of conviction.

> As we go through our tough seasons, as life demands more than we have, take position, stand firm with the power that comes from digging deep. Pushback with a 'come and take them' kind of attitude. What you believe in is bigger than you, and you need to use all the spiritual

truths revealed to you. In as much as the Greek army did not win the battle, at least they lost it after attempting to do something about it. Giving it their best fight and taking with them some life lessons, they gained an advantage as they knew what to do better next time. Even after their king died, the following year they did successfully expel the Persian invaders.[47]

As I chose to continue my walk armed with the teachings from my different struggles, with the Lord as my guide, even when I was surrounded, I believed that the best days were yet to come. As Sarah Reeves sings in 'Best Days':[48]

"As long as you got breath in your lungs,
This could be what dreams are made of".

> ♫ **To listen to the song:**
> https://www.youtube.com/watch?v=7ID1x0XsLyA

The choice of attitude is yours for the taking. What will it be for you?

In another praise and thanks anthem of mine, 'Reckless Love', there is a word of encouragement from the singer, Steffany Gretzinger, who stresses how it's not your pushing but the positioning of your heart that is the source of power in life's challenges.

> ♫ **To listen to the song:**
> https://youtu.be/zQIFJtBe2hA

Often we sing to prophesy until we believe, until we see something come to pass. There is something that happens when we shift our awareness from fear, when we move from that unloved place and fix our attention on the one who walks on water, the one who calls us beloved, who has been singing over us through all of time.

It's not in your push.

I noted this to myself: It most certainly was not in all the tactics I pushed to sell the house or my personal effort trying to resolve the different psychological and emotional conflicts with my ex. You can push with your own might, but soon enough you will be drained. You're not strong enough to push that far – it's not in your push, but it's in your position. As Steffany Gretzinger said,[49] "Position yourself inside of love". Let the "confidence that you are loved by the one who created you" straighten your back to stand tall in the day. Let love take hold of you, "deeper than anything else" that's had a hold of you. I believe it is from my position to receive this kind of love that I got the boost to pick myself up, dust myself off and keep on walking.

I once saw a preacher demonstrate the supernatural power of God and how it gives us strength to deal with the weight of the world. The preacher had two cans of Coke. One was empty, representing an empty vessel, that was not plugged into, or positioned in, the power of God, and another was full. When someone was called to step on the empty can, it went flying off the stage and eventually, when he got to it, he crushed it. When the same person stepped on the full one, he managed to balance himself on a small can of Coke. The same can is said to have the ability to hold about 340 kilograms (around 750 pounds) of weight. With our position in God as we plug into his supernatural, we, too, can bear the heavy weight of our challenges without even realising it.

In that period of listening to the song 'Reckless Love', I got a lovely message of encouragement from one of my close friends. Praise may not shift our circumstances, but it will begin to change our hearts.

'You are inspirational because despite your circumstances you have the capacity to love others (I don't even know what she was referring to here as I felt mostly disabled and very dependent on others during this period, but I accepted the praise anyway. She must have seen something I had missed!). The joy of the Lord is your strength. You are gold ... just going through the refining. This is not your destination. It is just a stop on the way. Our God is good, and his ways are higher than our ways – have a good day.'

So many times, we look at our problems and wish they never happened, but we wouldn't be who we are created to be without them. The writer and preacher, Joyce Meyer[50] looks at all the pain from her childhood abuse and all the problems it caused in her life. She hated that it happened and the people who did it, but all this hatred did was ruin her life as it led to more problems. Now, she doesn't know whether she can say she is sorry it all happened because that tragedy is what made her who she is today. She has a relationship with Jesus now and gives thanks as what she thought was her greatest enemy became her greatest friend.

We just need to trust God and let him get us to where we have a great testimony that will enable us to encourage somebody who is going through something tough in their life. Joyce decided that she wasn't going under but over and would survive. Although she hadn't had a good start in life, she intended to have a good finish.

Joseph is one of the best examples in the Bible of someone who had many unfair things happen to him yet chose to be made stronger. (Genesis 37) As I discussed earlier, when Joseph's master's wife took a liking to him and seduced him, he rejected her advances. But she then claimed he tried to rape her, and he was thrown in prison. Nothing is as annoying as making the right decision and getting the wrong result or seeing those who are doing the wrong thing seem to be blessed. It is one of the hardest things to endure.

Joseph was in slavery for about thirteen years and spent two years of that time in prison for something he didn't do. When the King Pharaoh had a dream that disturbed him, somebody finally remembered Joseph and that he had a gift for divining dreams. The king called him, and he was able to interpret the dream. As a result, he got promoted to second in command to the King of Egypt. He was put in a position that oversaw all the food during a seven-year famine. When his father and the brothers who were cruel to him came looking for food, he revealed who he was, and the siblings were afraid. They thought that he would kill them, but he said, "As for you, you meant evil against me, but God meant it for good, to bring it about that many people should be kept alive, as they are today." (Genesis 50:20 ESV)

Life point:

"Hardships prepare ordinary people for an extraordinary destiny."

C.S. Lewis

Dealing with Difficult Times

Don't waste your pain or let the things you have been through give you a bad attitude but ask God to use them to be a blessing for you and of help to somebody else. God is the alpha and omega, the beginning and the end = he knows everything from the very beginning and how it's going to turn out.

How can difficult times be made easier:

- stop trying to figure it out

- avoid excessive reasoning – even when you think you've got something figured out, you're probably not right

- we all want an explanation of what God gives us as the incarnation. He sent Jesus Christ who then left his Spirit to be in us should we choose to invite him into our lives. It was God and Christ reconciling the world and himself. He is always faithful. All we need to know is that God is love. He is with us; he loves us, and his word is true.

Joyce Meyer posed a question in a rather hilarious but very true manner that resonated with me and my trials. "How many of you think you are going through a test right now? Can I give you a word of encouragement – why don't you go ahead and pass it, so you don't have to take it again and again?"[51]

It took her about twenty years to grasp this. She didn't want to live the rest of her life going round and round the same stupid mountains and so she stood by God and said, "Let's get this over with". She found her way out through Christ by giving him praise, glory and honour. I chose to depend on Christ not myself. Depending on and trusting in something or someone greater is key.

You don't know what you believe until you have your faith tested. It's easy to have all the faith scriptures underlined, but that doesn't mean you are walking in faith. It is when you face the difficulties you get to really see.

Being Glad

Enjoying life depends on the attitude you decide to have towards it. Stay hopeful that this, too, will pass, and you won't get more than you can bear.

I certainly can attest that it is true that God is going to:

- work it all out
- work it out for good
- ensure all the challenges in your life serve a purpose
- make tomorrow better.

All this is to keep you motivated – don't give up! Even when *the how* might be very foggy.

Like Pollyanna – a character in a Disney movie of the same name from many years ago – Joyce Meyer[52] loves to play the Glad Game to upset the enemy by finding something to be happy about. The game will have you looking for something good no matter the situation.

I found that, at the peak of my challenges, starting 30 days of gratitude helped. Each day I looked for at least three items to be grateful for during my day from morning to evening. It was a good nudge in the right direction and helped me combat depression.

Pollyanna first learned of the Glad Game when she got crutches that she had no use for mistakenly donated as a gift to her instead of a doll that she had asked for. To get her to forget and not be sad, her poor father played the game with her, forcing her to think of the things she was glad about instead. Soon enough, her attitude started to change.

After the death of her parents, Pollyanna ended up moving towns to live with her aunt. She shared the Glad Game with all those she came across. She would say or make time to do something worth their while to leave them with a positive attitude. Without realising, she changed several people's lives.

Unfortunately, Pollyanna had a fall, and her legs became paralysed. When she found out the news, she started slipping into depression. Her doctor was concerned that, if there was no change with the depression, then the highly risky procedure to get her legs to function again would be more complicated.

Playing the game now seemed silly to Pollyanna, and nothing was appealing. When she had visitors, she needed to be forced out of bed. The people she had made an impact on filled up her aunt's courtyard and foyer as they all came to wish her well. They each told her how she had made a difference in their lives, which lifted her spirit.

Making each day count and not wasting our day doesn't mean being busy every minute. It does mean – have a plan, work your plan and put time into that which will bear good fruit. You don't want to get to the end of the day and be frustrated that a day has passed and you don't know what you did with it.

Thanks and Praise in the Midst of Adversity

As I went about my day to day amidst all my challenges, I came across a teaching on thanksgiving in adversity by Dr Charles Stanley[53] that serves as a reminder that you are walking in Jesus's presence, and you are not doing it alone. When going through heartache, turmoil or the loss of someone we love, be aware in his presence and in everything give thanks because it gets you to pause and ask yourself: How does God view this? What does he promise me? How is he going to work in this situation or circumstance?

What giving thanks does:

1. When you start the day, you are aware that you walk in his Presence and whatever happens in the day, happens in the presence of a Holy God who lives inside of you.

2. If you are grateful, you will look for his presence – sometimes he reveals his purpose, sometimes he doesn't. At times we don't expect what happens and are in shock, but that doesn't mean He forgot you; even when you don't understand his purpose, he will turn the worst kind of things for good.

   Say "God, I don't like or understand this hurt/loss and it doesn't go with what I think about you, but I am going to trust you. I am going to thank you and love you despite anything I feel". Perhaps you don't think that's true, but you will only find out when you do it. God is the same when things are good or bad and he keeps his promise.

3. It brings us to submission to his will. When I'm going through something painful emotionally or physically, it does something to my hurt or pain when I'm able to thank him. Even when you don't feel the heart of gratitude, just say it. God fully understands humanity and he doesn't play favourites. He keeps his word to all of us no matter who we are.

4. It reminds us of our continuing dependence upon him. Everything might be fine one moment and might change the next moment, but the one thing that doesn't change is God. No matter what happens, as a child of God, he will see you through it.

5. It helps us trust him even when we don't understand why. All of us have been through circumstances where we ask *why*? He never promises to tell us why, but he does promise to be with us no matter what, to enable us to walk. Thanksgiving reminds me to remember the fact that I must be obedient in the process.

6. It is essential in our rejoicing during suffering. If I am going to rejoice realistically, I've got to thank him. The pain, suffering, hurt you might be going through maybe so deep, penetrating, and so

exhausting that when you tell God you are grateful, but you don't really feel it, God understands how you feel. When your physical pain shouts louder than you can speak, one thing for sure is God hears you, though nobody else can. You can thank him no matter what. Thank him with your lips until you can thank him with your heart, soul, spirit – your very being. He understood what Jesus was feeling when he was stretched out, nailed on the cross and cried out in pain "My God, my God why have you forsaken me?" (Matthew 27:46 and Mark 15:34 NIV)

7. It gives our testimony greater impact. When I can say "Thank you, God, for difficult times" there is something about our witness and our testimony that changes. When you say to someone you know "I've been there", or "I know what it means to walk in your steps and I understand why you don't believe, or why you are hurting or don't want to talk about God because that's where I was", you fling the door open to other people, showing them there is someone who understands them.

8. It helps displace our own anxiety with peace. As we saw earlier, 'peace' in Greek = to bind together and so when I think about the peace of God, we are bound together with him, in his presence and power. When we are able to thank him the anxiety crumbles within us and peace prevails. We might still be feeling a certain way physically or emotionally, but there is an overwhelming sense of indescribable peace that comes from an intimate relationship with Jesus Christ.

9. It teaches us to focus on him, not the circumstances. This is something that is very hard to do, especially when we are really hurting, and something is going on inside. If you focus on circumstances, the pain becomes more unbearable. Peace will elude you, and nothing will seem to work out right. Focus on his word and you will find peace and thanksgiving.

Low or Bitter Spirit?

If you're feeling low or bitter, it's a clue you have forgotten these words: **Thanks** and **Praise**. Search for them in the Word, prayer, song, writing or however you can until your soul is at rest.

Start giving thanks even when you are not where you should be. Asking why – why this happened to you, why that person did this, are not the relevant or right questions to ask yourself. Instead, ask: What did I learn from this? What can I do to better myself? Give thanks for the *what*. With the *why* you fall in the negative and become powerless and with the *what* you fall in the positive and become powerful. You can choose to either be low, bitter, and beaten down from the 'why' or learn from the 'what' of where you are right now to rebuild yourself. People are not interested in failures as they have plenty of their own to keep them up at night, but they are interested in *what* you did to survive those failures to give them hope and a blueprint on what to do to work on their own issues.

No matter what my world looks like, I need to remember that I don't have to thank God for the bad times but thank him for being there because he has proven his faithfulness time after time even when there was no hope. He is with me and turns the mourning into dancing. This is not only in my life or Bible story times, but in the lives of people living in my time, people I know personally and others whose stories I have come to know through their telling and publishing.

It is important to learn to give thanks in the middle of anything you might be walking through. This is an obvious message when things are going well, but it's easy to slip into the negative when things aren't, as was the case for Pollyanna when she was paralysed. This is when we need to remind ourselves of the goodness in giving thanks, praise or playing the Glad Game and rely on our support network for a boost to work on the 'what'.

It started looking up for Pollyanna when she listened to what all those who used to be in a negative space had to say. With Pollyanna's improvement in spirit, her doctor was happier for her to undergo the operation on her legs. I imagine from then on, as long as she kept working on herself and staying positive, she would have built even more resilience than before when she managed to help one person at a time in her aunt's little town.

I once heard a preacher say that most of the great things you are going to do in your life, you would not understand, see coming, pick or want to happen, so just keep on keeping on. At times, God starts to do something you don't feel, but you are in it to follow him and give thanks for his ways. His thoughts are higher than yours (Isaiah 55).

Choose to "Trust in the LORD with all your heart and lean not on your own understanding, in all your ways acknowledge Him, And He shall direct your paths." (Proverbs 3 NKJV)

We already know the overall result is for our good. We need to learn to embrace '**no**' in life. We need to recognise that '**no**' = 'k**no**wledge'. We don't have the details of the form our 'no' will take, whether it will be giants, mountains, valleys or closed doors. If we knew, we would probably get comfortable where we are and opt not to go through the challenges.

Thirty Days of Gratitude

My 30 days of gratitude was part of my quest to change my outlook and seek ways to have a thankful heart no matter how good or bad the days were. I had made a choice to rise from my fall and ground myself in the Father. When trouble seemed in hot pursuit of me, there is a point in time I questioned – where is God during it all? As I sought to give thanks, I came across a Joseph Prince sermon.[54] He encouraged us to thank God for our experiences, education, background and the like but not to depend on our smarts. Looking at the story of Esther, he paints a picture of how God works in the background to save his people from a death sentence when they are in captivity.

We tend to give thanks and praise to God for the help we are aware of, but there are often times he protects behind the scenes. I know this to be true as I have seen near miss accidents with people who are blissfully unaware of how close they were to a disaster and don't know to give thanks for that escape.

In the book of Esther, we see how favours saw Esther through, and eventually saved her and her people from death.

Esther's story took place in the time of Xerxes, who ruled from India to Ethiopia – 127 provinces in all. King Xerxes ruled from his royal throne in the palace complex of Susa (Esther 1).[55] He held a beauty contest to replace Queen Vashti.

> "8 … many young women were brought to the citadel of Susa and put under the care of Hegai. Esther also was taken to the king's palace … 9 She pleased him and won his favor … 15 Esther won the favor of everyone who saw her. 17 Now the king was attracted to Esther more than to any of the other women, and she won his favor and approval more than any of the other virgins. So, he set a royal crown on her head and made her queen instead of Vashti." (Esther 2 NIV)

When Haman, a palace official, came up with a plan to have Mordecai – Queen Esther's relative and all the Jews killed – as I discussed earlier when I talked about my own experience fasting – Esther fasted and prayed with her people. She then went before the king to request to save her people, and with favour, it was granted.

By putting our faith in God with his grace and favour we can get our breakthrough, just like Esther and Mordecai did. With our hope in him we are blessed.

Bright Moments in the Dark

I continued to look for thank you(s) and favour in my life.

At one point during the house selling debacle, a finalist of the Australian reality TV show *House Rules* – Danielle – responded to my email requesting any sort of help to sell the house and be paid upon sale. Yes, I did get that desperate and tested all means outside the box. For me, the fact that she took the time to respond, although unable to physically come and help, was a sign of God's spirit moving in my favour.

During my period of hardship, I received a repayment of a debt I had written off almost ten years before. It was in Godspeed and perfect timing. It put me in good standing to keep up with mortgage repayments and other property selling costs at a time I needed it the most in my life when I was facing possible repossession of the biggest asset I had ever owned if I defaulted on payments.

Not only that, there was an extra government payment that came through at the most unexpected time. I only realised it a few days later and I was blown away as I wrote down – "Oh wow, how God works. He knew that he already had me covered with this! ... Thank you, Lord. It's like assurance to say to me 'though there is loud silence with the house sale, you are here with me, and you will make the big move soon!'"

Although at this point I still hadn't sold the house, I could see the wind of God's mercy and favour in motion for action. It was blowing in my direction to fight my battles. I was learning to tune in to recognise his voice when he spoke and filter out the voices that were not his.

Another bright light in the dark was my dad. I was thankful for him working on an emergency passport and making arrangements to visit. He had to renew his passport in Zimbabwe, which normally would take months even without the pandemic in the picture. He sent through a text message saying how amazing that God's favour abounds even in chaos. In less than a fortnight his passport was ready for collection. He put his life on hold for months on end to be there for me for as long as I needed help. Throughout my different challenges he stood in prayer with me, with the Bible in hand to fight the battle. He pointed out to me that being intentional about giving thanks and standing in faith in the Lord amid the chaos was for my own good. In his exact words:

> "Let us commit this before the Lord three times a day: morning, afternoon, and evening with thanksgiving. God Almighty has plans for you. (Jeremiah 29:11) Though you are in a crucible of very hard knocks, he indeed is refining you to more than the purest gold, before he puts you on a pedestal. Trust him, he is faithful and has unfailing love and great compassion. Believe him for this gift to manifest."

With the undeserved favour I received, not because of anything I had done, but simply because I was loved, I stood in the middle of my chaos to give thanks to the Lord because of his righteousness and sing the praises of the name of the Lord Most High (Psalms 7:17). To cope with my failures and challenges, I felt the spirit led me to read the Easter story of Jesus, the foundation of my faith. It felt as if in my situation, I was in the tomb with him. Physically, death appeared to be the end, failure of all, including the belief in God … But it wasn't. It was just a period of waiting for the spirit to do its work, and on the third day, there was a resurrection. Jesus rose again.

"It's soon"– I kept hearing the gentle voice of the Spirit as the physical situation in my life looked even worse than before (and the time frame to see a turnaround with the house sale was not three calendar days!).

A message in my pop-up verse:

> "He will swallow up death in victory" (Isaiah 25:8 King James Version (KJV)).

Hallelujah!

After the keen buyers' Christmas and New Year holiday getaway, which had seemed like an eternity for me, they finally responded in writing. Their final written offer was $100,000 lower than the very first verbal offer I had during the home's first campaign but also higher than the offer from the second campaign after the auction. My realtor had asked for their best offer and that was their maximum increase, for which I was grateful.

In April 2020, finally the house sold!

My real estate agent presented a final written offer that ended up being fifteen thousand dollars above the original offer. When this happened, I was on the verge of not only facing repossession as I was running out of finances to meet the monthly repayments, but I was also facing yet another property court case with all the uncertainty that came with this new unknown Covid-19 worldwide pandemic. I had faced one challenge after the other. Just in the nick of time it was as if the sale happened overnight (well, 'two years overnight'). I suppose God was done with the lessons I had to learn in that season as he prepared me for the next season's challenges stronger than before. A contract got signed and finalised successfully this time.

Having that big bold 'SOLD' sign I had longed to see in front of our house was like sweet victory. It had taken bucket loads, if not a mini river of tears, sweat and blood, to get there.

Frank, the realtor and colleague for life, had encouraged me not to give up by faithfully keeping at it. He stuck that sold sign with me with as much joy as I had as we basked in the light at the end of the long, winding tunnel we had been through together. We took a moment to share a bottle of champagne in celebration, reminiscing on our University of Life experiences. It was indeed just like an actual graduation.

I wrote an announcement of joy and thanks to my family and friends:

'I appreciate all your prayers and support because I know I would not be where I am standing now without them. God is the source and uses people and other resources to get you there. I appreciate it from the bottom of my heart. I have seen and I see God's hand in the mess as he creates a message, and I could never deny that He exists no matter the lions' den I have been in.'

In good and Godspeed simultaneously, my family ended up in an available, much smaller house. I even managed to arrange to rent the place first and use some of that rental money as part of the purchase. This was indeed another miracle in itself, considering how rent-to-buy was not much of a trend in Australia in 2020.

Resettling worked out perfectly in many ways for both my daughter and me in terms of day care, school, plus proximity to our support network. I now had answers to the drawn-out concerns I had for my girl's transition from the matrimonial home. Despite the challenges and feeling like I was walking on fire or in a lion's den, his love conquered all. I saw myself as chosen and loved. I could see God for who he is in all his glory, love and faithfulness.

"God sends forth his love and faithfulness ... 4 I am in the midst of lions; I am forced to dwell among ravenous beasts—... 7 My heart, O God, is steadfast, my heart is steadfast; I will sing and make music. 9 I will praise you, Lord, among the nations, I will sing of you among the peoples. 10 For great is your love, reaching to the heavens, your faithfulness reaches to the skies. 11 Be exalted, O God, above the heavens; let your glory be over all the earth." (Psalms 57:3-11 NIV)

Not that everything went completely smoothly from then on. It was one thing after another with the challenges and blessings of the sale, move and legal proceedings. After the good news of the sale that had taken years to come, my dad had a sudden finger infection and hospitalisation and then we had car issues (not to mention the car we borrowed broke down minutes into driving it). I just wanted to burst into tears at what seemed to me like an avalanche of attacks, but I resisted because I literally didn't even have time for that. I had to focus on dad's health in hospital, then deal with everything else after.

Issues with the move and the new house when the garage flooded (we had to put stuff for storage there as we unpacked), did not help the situation. It was like each step of progress was getting tallied up with a challenge. Despite it all, I most certainly saw the favour that came my way and above all, in the end God had come out on top in that lions' den. It's exactly as the song 'Defender' says, which I mentioned earlier in the book.[56] He is the ultimate Defender. I stand firm in my conviction and confidence today knowing not just from a song, but my own experience, that my God will never fail, and not only will I see a victory, but I have seen a victory![57]

The property issue era was coming to an end. I continued to leave the rest for him to fight for what's best with the greatest confidence in his way. I began to see the light not only in him but also in myself, depending on my choice or response to what happens in my life.

Jesus says, "I am the light of the world ..." (John 8:12 NIV)

"14 You are the light of the world. A town built on a hill cannot be hidden. 15 Neither do people light a lamp and put it under a bowl. Instead, they put it on its stand, and it gives light to everyone in the house. 16 In the same way, let your light shine before others, that they may see your good deeds and glorify your Father in heaven." (Matthew 5:14-16 NIV)

The Lord stood indeed as the 'Way Maker' and 'light in the darkness' as per one of my go-to songs throughout the journey – 'Way Maker'.

> ♫ **Listen to Way Maker by Osinachi Kalu Okoro Egbu:**
> https://www.youtube.com/watch?v=r1tW42hlVpA

My Gratitude

One of the biggest lessons I learned is that if you can't change your circumstances, then change yourself, and one of the biggest tools was changing my attitude with gratitude. As I mentioned, I started 30 days of journalling to give thanks and praise.

Looking back through this journal, even though times weren't the best for our family in the separation, there were also some nuggets of good days to be thankful for. There was a lovely sunny day that my ex made brunch whilst my daughter, her aunt and I had gone out. As we walked in the house, we appreciated the open doors bringing the outdoors indoors thinking it was all part of the beautiful brunch. It all looked just perfect. My ex then explained how he had burnt some ingredients and smoked out the house so had to open all the alfresco folding doors in the dining and lounge area. It turned out to be a beautiful disaster. He said something along the lines of how something terrible can result in something beautiful. It was a reiteration of what I had learned that morning about how the beauty of pearls comes from irritation, which I mentioned earlier in this book.

As I fought my battles, it literally felt like being in the fire. My saving grace was counting my blessings and the joys as I worked on growing my faith in God through readings plus praise and thanks music. I was challenged to pray in or out of my crisis.

In the book of Daniel 3, there is a story of Shadrach, Meshach and Abednego. They refused to bow down and worship the king's golden statue. If they had to be thrown into the fire for refusing and sticking to worshipping their true God, then so be it. They believed that their God would save them and even if he didn't, then they would still not do it. They were thrown into the fiery furnace and eventually were saved. It served as a reminder to worship and stand by God for who he is, not what he does, even during great trials when it seems he isn't there. There is a thanks and praise song on this theme, 'Another in the Fire':[58] "Even if he doesn't (I ain't changing my confession or my belief or who I believe in)."

> ♫ **To listen to the song:**
> https://youtu.be/zmNc0L7Ac5c

As I went through the fire, the song 'See a Victory'[59] is another praise and worship song that strengthened me. I wore it as mine as I drew strength from how Shadrach, Meshach and Abednego were literally saved in the fire. Standing to see a victory I declared: "I'm gonna see a victory For the battle belongs to You Lord."

> ♫ **To listen to the song:**
> https://www.youtube.com/watch?v=YNd-PbVhnvA

Through all my trials and tribulations, I always found grace and favour. Having parental care of my daughter 24/7 also meant I didn't miss any milestones, her comedy and the joy she brings; we still had a roof over our heads, a place she was familiar with as we looked to move to the next phase of our life, and I had a job to wake up to, to support us financially and a great support network in different people. Through the triumphs big or small – our miracle baby girl, gift of life, moving on, resettling in our new home, learning to walk again and standing still, I learned to thank God for who he is.

His voice is the one I chose as my guide. In it I felt him say he is for us, and he is with us through it all. We will bear fruit because in him we are planted in rich soil.

From the book of Psalms:

> "2 ... whose delight is in the law of the Lord,
> and who meditates on his law day and night.
> 3 That person is like a tree planted by streams of water,
> which yields its fruit in season
> and whose leaf does not wither—
> whatever they do prospers." (Psalm 1:2-3 NIV)

'O Taste and See'[60] was also a go-to song for me that gave me joy through it all. When I saw my victories, I truly felt the promise to turn my mourning into dance and my sadness to joy come to life, and I danced to it with a different leap. I sang and danced my heart out in joy, and I hope the same for you also, that you get to encounter him, to taste and see him. My story and living my life are my thanks to him.

> ♫ **To listen to the song:**
> https://www.youtube.com/watch?v=Ry2u9hmIUoM

"You turned my wailing into dancing; you removed my sackcloth and clothed me with joy." (Psalms 30:11 NIV)

The fall is not what defines us but how we rise from the fall. This point came together for me through Carolanne Miljavac's[61] devotion. When we are broken, our knees hit the pavement and our faces rest on the ground where his voice is the only sound. From there, how we then choose to define ourselves is in how we rise, and I chose to do so grounded in our Father.

Carolanne poses a question – have you been too distracted to see God's glory? Sometimes we need to be humbled enough to see him. When the enemy has stripped our sanity, God shows up and shows off. That is what's so jump-up-and-down exhilarating about being a child of God. Every scheme of the enemy only brings us that much closer to realising who we belong to and in our brokenness, God can finally be the strength in our weakness. This realisation is a reason to be grateful and give praise.

As I said earlier, when I was lost and at my weakest, I questioned everything from the beginning about my identity. I realised that ultimately, I am a child of God, so I am who he says I am, and I am forever grateful for that.

> ♫ **To listen to the song and read the lyrics of (I Am) Who You Say I Am, which I find inspiring:**
> https://hillsong.com/lyrics/who-you-say-i-am/

How to Be Grateful with a Heavy Heart

At times, I felt heavy as I looked for something to be grateful for in my 30 days of gratitude. There was one such morning that I went down on my knees to pray with such a heavy heart; I wasn't even sure how to start the day, let alone get through it. My sweet little girl came to me and said, "It's okay, Mummy." I thought I didn't hear her right, but she repeated it, "It's okay, Mummy. I love you." She then wrapped her tiny arms around me to give me a big hug! They were just the right words and actions from the smallest of people at the right time. That is what I had to be thankful for on that day. It made me feel lighter and kept me putting one foot in front of the other. It goes to show how even random small acts of kindness through a few words or just a simple hug can save the day for someone.

When I looked back, this is not the only time I got some comfort from my little girl's cleverness, outlook in life, kindness and humour. On one particular day, as I took a break from the mowing, she came outside at the right time with just the right words to cheer me on: "Mummy, you can do it!" Then she clapped her little hands with the biggest smile.

Behind the rows of houses on the opposite side of the road were power lines out in the bush that stopped a prospective buyer from making an offer. A little while after this my daughter pointed them out to me very excitedly as the Eiffel Tower! Lol! Clearly, that buyer missed out on the view of a lifetime! She gave me a good laugh and that was just the medicine my soul needed.

She went through a phase where she loved to give me a rub on the cheek, kisses and a big squeeze or cuddle. I got the true definition of 'my little bundle of joy', and I was grateful to God for this gift of life.

As I aimed to wash away my heavy spirit, I looked for a way to cling onto the lighter spirit I had found through my daughter's words of encouragement and actions. Being the person that I am, I started off with breaking down my status at the time.

Issue: Spirit of heaviness and struggling to use the weapons of praise (Kudzai) and thanks (Tinotenda) that I know I should be using.

If you struggle with this same heaviness, then there are some tips to help you. I came across an article by Kimberly Taylor with practical ways to lift the spirit of heaviness.[62]

What is heaviness? In Hebrew it is *keheh*, which means "dim, dull or faint." In Matthew 5:14 Jesus refers to believers as "light of the world" and so with life's challenges the enemy works to have this light go dim, dull or faint.

Kimberly draws on Isaiah 61:3, which I held as one of my earlier promises from God. It warns us of the existence of the heavy spirit, but there is also hope in scripture on how to deal with it.

"To console those who mourn in Zion, To give them beauty for ashes, The oil of joy for mourning, The garment of praise for the spirit of heaviness; That they may be called trees of righteousness, The planting of the LORD, that He may be glorified." (Isaiah 61:3 NKJV)

The garment of praise for the spirit of heaviness is key, and something I learned earlier on, and yet I still sometimes struggle with it.

Why the spirit of heaviness?

Cause: It helps to pinpoint the underlying cause first, and then you will understand why the methods to lift it work.

Kimberly, who suffered from depression herself, learned from a psychiatrist that the struggle with depression or anxiety is **linked to a habit of fault-finding**, where the focus is on what is wrong and what is lacking.

What we are urged to practice: I was encouraged to look at

- spirit discernment, which requires
- awareness of the thoughts that are directing focus and
- ensure they line up with my beliefs (for me, this is in the word of God, that is, the report of what he says.)

I took the time to pause my unsettled spirit by writing down questions and answers to see where I was at in that moment since it had been pointed out that the cause was linked to focusing on faults – the worst within oneself, other people or in one's life situation. I found going through the process step by step as I wrote it down helped with my work on the spirit and perspective.

Q. What do you focus on?

For example,

Do you focus on fault within yourself or others?

A.

No, that was not the cause for me in that case and at that stage of my life.

I didn't blame myself or any other person. I had even come to learn that the enemy doesn't cause all situations we are in, nor does God allow them, so blaming the devil or God was not on my radar either. Even if it was something that happened to me without my doing, I had the option to choose how I responded to it and my way forward from there. I had learned to take time to consult with the spirit before making any decisions, to own my choices fully, and whether the results were good or bad, to note what works but especially learn from what doesn't.

Do you focus on what is wrong and what is lacking?

A.

Yes, that seemed to be more the case in that instance. I had zoomed in on how I

- had no written offers after multiple premier advertising campaigns done in hope and faith
- had savings running out
- was tired of all my responsibilities, physical or financial.

Solution: Praise and Thanks

Kimberly substantiated Isaiah 61:3 for me saying that reading this scripture reminds us that a garment is something that we must put on intentionally; after all, our clothes don't put themselves on!

The following are three ways to put on the garment of praise every day that I chose to follow through with:

How to do this practically: especially when the spirit is heavy.

1. **Listen, sing** to praise and worship music regularly.

   This could be when doing chores, driving and the like. Also, have moments of keeping still to just listen, reflect and journal. I found at the start of the day setting aside some time for meditation based on the word of God was necessary to help redirect my day to his faithfulness and give hope.

2. **Create a gratitude list.**

Using the scripture as a prescription:

"Seven times a day I praise you for your righteous laws." (Psalms 119:164 NIV)

As I chose to keep going with my thanks and praise items each day for my 30 days of gratitude journey that I had started, I found that forced me to change focus and look for or see what was going right each day. Even if it was someone giving way for me, a compliment from a stranger when I was out and about, or if someone said something funny that made me laugh. I started noting down not just the big but also the little things that happened in and around me throughout the day be it with family, friends, colleagues, other people within my support network or random people.

With this habit I recorded how I appreciated even a day at the beach with my daughter and friends that I would normally look at as business as usual without fully appreciating its beauty. I also noted how I went to my local hardware store expecting to pay for a battery replacement for my garden tool. With the help of the Bunnings staff – Jo and Kylie – I was super amazed instead because I got the whole Whipper Snipper replaced with another brand new one. They explained to me that the battery had a separate three-year warranty and the Whipper Snipper itself had five years. I had no idea since I had bought it a few years back and lost track of the details, but they sure brightened up my day.

"Give thanks in all circumstances, for this is God's will for you in Christ Jesus." (1 Thessalonians 5:18 NIV)

Each day aim to set your heart on praise and thanksgiving. To build a habit, see if you can set aside a period to do it. You could start today by doing it each day for one week, then one month and see how you go.

3. **Write a 'thank you' note** to all the people on your gratitude list

You could commit yourself to writing a brief thank you note a day per person to let them know how much you appreciate them. This helps shift focus to the positive. It cultivates praise by replacing the fault-finding that brings on the spirit of heaviness with finding praise in others or the situation.

I took the time to thank all the different people on my list in different ways, which lifted my spirit as I got to see clearly how truly blessed I was.

Learning to Focus

As I continued my gratitude journey with extra tools, I had a lot more to be easily grateful for and to focus on, even during the rainy days. I took note of everything big and small, focusing on the moment. I started by looking at how grateful I was for having God in my life. Then I focused on how my day went as I dropped off my daughter at day care, appreciating all the staff and her carers. I was grateful for my workmates and the teamwork and for my friends and family who would not only babysit but also do the pickup when I needed help for house inspections, work or just alone time.

I was thankful for all the teachings on focus that I learned and around the same time there was coincidentally a movie called, *The Art of Racing in the Rain* (based on the novel of the same name) that enlightened me further. It tells the story of a driver named Denny whose life is told from observations by his dog, Enzo. If it rained, it didn't seem like it rained for Denny on the corners of the racecourse. He skidded the car before it could skid. He took note of how the best race car drivers focus only on the present, without dwelling on the past or committing to the future. Reflection must come later, which is why race car drivers will compulsively record their every move during the race. If a driver has the courage to create his own conditions, then the rain is simply rain.

So why did this resonate with me? Because I had realised that, ultimately, I am responsible for myself, and I need to keep learning skills to be the best driver of my life. Consistently recording the good things, the thanks and praise for that day as it happened, helped keep the focus in that moment and not the past or future. Like Denny, I found myself having the ability to essentially 'skid the car before it skidded'.

The thanks and praise automatically got me to fight the challenges, staying on top of them instead of them getting on top of me. This, in turn, helped me get through the rainy or stormy days. The reflection that came later after all was said and done got me leaning on the other ten spiritual affirmations I learned: listen, believe, have faith, be humble and at peace, have confidence, patience and courage, forgive and love. I had what I needed to navigate my own life as the best driver and to look at the rain as simply rain.

When I reined in my focus on only the present, taking it one moment, step or day at a time, I managed to take hold of and handle what was going on in my life instead of being overwhelmed by it. During the house sale struggles, I found myself putting aside thoughts that made me disheartened, such as the past house sale record, having no offers or that my funds were running low and focusing on only that day. On such days, I wrote to myself things like, 'Today I am winning – I got the mortgage paid off for this month. The house is on the first page of the advertising listing. I have a support network praying and rooting for me. My daughter and I are in good health, with food, shelter, each other, had quality time – with morning talk, cuddles, dancing, swimming, playing at the park'.

With random people I encountered, I found goodness when I didn't take it for granted.

I had a God who repeated – don't be afraid, don't be discouraged. His mercies are new every morning (Lamentations 3). And yes, each morning or day I took the time to listen and look at his mercies; my focus stayed on track.

"Starve your distractions feed, your focus."

Anon

This is a quote I found later that complemented my thinking. Digging in on it helped me take action to starve what was distracting me and find my way back to feeding my focus. It exposed a wealth of practical lessons to share. On one particular day, I realised my distractions were linked to anger, fault-finding with others and mostly towards myself for not achieving my goals. Despite others being a very small factor, the main issue was a social media platform I was using. I decided it was best for me to physically remove it from my phone for a time frame to help redirect my focus on achieving my writing goals and spending better quality time in my relationships with those around me.

I felt even more relieved and grateful as I came across some practical teachings by Leon Ho (founder and CEO of Lifehack)[63] to help me stay on point with what I had already actioned by identifying three good things about my day, my focus and what I feed it.

Leon highlights how an awareness of where we spend our time and energy is important as it's linked to where our focus goes. If this is going to distractions, then we need to make the necessary changes so we direct our time and energy towards thoughts and actions that feed our goals and dreams. I believe we essentially need to do a stocktake of what we are feeling, thinking and actioning. This is how I came to recognise that my anger was linked to my fault-finding thoughts. This led me to delete the social media app (where I spent too much time venting) from my phone. It seemed to be the root cause of the negative feelings or thoughts.

Leon highlights how starving distractions of our time plus energy then naturally feeds our focus, which, in turn, increases productivity and success. He teaches us to ask ourselves certain questions and take some actions:

What are your distractions?

There are two types:

- **External** – which come from a source outside you. These come from social media apps linked to the phone, calls, texts, news and the like.

- **Internal** – which come from your own thoughts and emotions. These are to do with, say, in my case, the fault-finding and anger that was linked to my phone app interaction.

  In relation to emotions, if there is stress, depression or anxiety, then it is an uphill battle to rein in that energy and those thoughts to focus on what needs to be done, but it can be done. Applying tools already learned, plus leaning on my support network, including professional help from therapists, was my game changer.

A combination of both external and internal distractions is a perfect recipe for disaster, and you are unlikely to achieve your goals on time and efficiently, so you must prompt yourself further to get there.

How do you stop distractions and start focusing?

Action must be taken with immediate effect to work on stopping distractions:

- **External distractions** – need to be nipped in the bud to help feed focus.

  This can consist of temporarily deleting a phone app, like I did. You can work on committing yourself to a time frame as you gauge your progress or efficiency to focus on the tasks at hand.

- **Internal distractions** – affirmations, habits, tools or exercises and your support network (as detailed earlier in this book) based on what it is you are struggling with will be of help to work on internal distractions. For example, undertaking exercises, such as 'Giving thanks with a heavy heart' – help with finding or feeding focus.

You can create a vision and action board to follow through. I keep my action boards as simple as the examples in 1 and 2 below.

Leon highlights some 'how to' stop distractions steps:[64]

1. **Eliminate Options** – by narrowing down the distractions and tallying them against an action item. I have added an example of my focus items to achieve, along with what kept me distracted externally and internally. Below is how I tackled them, adapting the original example to suit my situation and the steps I had already taken:

	FOCUS	DISTRACTION	HOW TO ELIMINATE
	Example: Administration work	Checking friends' group phone text messages	Silence phone (other options – lock it away or turn it off)
1	Writing project	External – checking and interacting on social media app on phone	Uninstall the app > zoomed in on thanksgiving on the dream of achieving the project plus the impact it would have by saying thanks out loud at the start of my morning thanksgiving
2	Quality time with loved ones	Internal – stirred up anger, fault-finding with others & mostly myself, arising from the external interaction on phone	Attitude of gratitude – said out loud in thanksgiving and wrote down three good things I appreciated about my loved ones and good times we have when in a positive space

2. **Create stop signs in your mind** – setting mental stop signs for yourself can also help with ending distractions.

	FOCUS	DISTRACTION	STOP SIGN
	Example: Administration work	Web surfing	Set timer or use Focus Timer on your computer to stop after, say, ten minutes
1	Writing project	Surfing social media app on phone	Committed to staying away from the uninstalled app for one full day for a start. (My intention was to extend that to a week or until my writing project progressed to the next stage that required outsourcing)

A lesson I have learned is that no one, including yourself, should distract you from focusing on achieving your goals.

Will You Use Your Past or Will Your Past Continue to Use you?

This was a question posed in one of the teachings I came across. What we all have in common is a past where we have made mistakes, even some that only we are aware of. It is how we use that past that differentiates us. If the past didn't kill us, then we need to use it as a weapon of mass destruction against struggles.

It was through my bad experiences that my weaknesses were exposed and called for my attention. I would otherwise have lived without ever knowing or acknowledging them and not growing into the fullness of who I am meant to be. I understand better now that I have found my way back to a personal relationship with God. His power is made perfect in my weakness; therefore, I will boast more gladly about my weaknesses. I learned to cherish my weaknesses, insults, hardships, persecutions and difficulties, for when I am weak, then I am strong. (2 Corinthians 12)

When asked what he is most proud of, Brett Clark[65] tells a story of how as parents, he and his wife Maria dealt with the tragedy of losing their premature, one-week-old daughter. They turned it into something positive. They raised funds in her memory that helped other premature babies win the battle their baby lost. Tragedy can affect us all, but it is how we deal with it that will shape our legacy.

After Jesus's resurrection and ascension – in the book of Acts 5 – Peter and the apostles went through towns working wonders and teaching about Jesus. Not everyone was happy about this, but even after the apostles were arrested, they continued to teach.

When asked why, they replied,

> "We must obey God rather than men. 30 The God of our fathers raised Jesus, whom you killed by hanging him on a tree. 31 God exalted him at his right hand as Leader and Saviour, to give repentance to Israel and forgiveness of sins. 32 And we are witnesses to these things, and so is the Holy Spirit, whom God has given to those who obey him." (Acts 5:29-32 ESV)

This enraged the council, who wanted to kill them. However, a teacher of the law held in honour by all the people had some advice for them. He pointed out how, in the past, other leaders who had followers were killed and the following came to nothing. He recommended that they leave Peter and the apostles alone, for if their work was of their own undertaking, then it would fail, but if it was of God, then they would not be able to overthrow them. If they did so, they would be fighting against God.

So, the apostles got a beating instead and were ordered not to speak in Jesus's name. They left rejoicing as they found worth in the suffering they had faced. They were freed and still went on with their teachings.

Thank God for your past, for if it didn't kill you, then you get to use it. The apostles gave thanks as they went from house to house, telling people what had happened, using the very weapon meant to destroy them as a story of their faith.

Are you being used by your past or using your past? There is a difference in the reflection. I learned that I had a choice to have either mine or Jesus's face in the reflection. It is not about the extraordinary people being used, but the ordinary ones just like me who have faults and weaknesses, who refuse to be defined by their failure but by their saviour instead.

Triumph in Challenges

I was challenged by a statement I once heard on being marred by challenges but exalted by triumphs.[66] Based on how we choose to apply the challenges, they could be a source of our triumph to be grateful for and not the bane of our existence. In my search, I came across Mark S Brown's[67] and Ashley Lee's[68] work on triumph over challenges and living in the moment with success and failure. If we want success and to experience triumph, then we must act.

How do you handle a setback?

Do you let it rule your day or even your whole week? Does it ruin all the progress you have made already?

Many of us need to learn how to handle failures better and reap the lessons learned from them instead.

Fear of failure is a natural, human instinct. The best way to fight it is by embracing it! We must say to ourselves:

- failure is not a weakness but a starting off point for success.

- mistakes are what we use to anticipate and prevent future problems when we learn from them.

Without the setbacks, there would be little or no process improvements or service and product enhancements. With perfection from the get-go, we would never dare to push for creativity, innovation, rethink or reinvent and could find ourselves at a standstill instead. Thomas Edison is known for solutions needing modification including his biggest success with the incandescent light bulb.[69] He said,

"I have not failed 10,000 times—I've successfully found 10,000 ways that will not work."

What can you do to counteract stress?

The stress that comes along with fear of failure is described as enough to knock any of us flat on our backs.

Try writing down what you are grateful for in your life. A University of Miami study[70] has proven that **giving thanks instead of counting burdens can ease stress.**

There is an old song I used to sing at Sunday school in my younger days, 'Count your blessings' by Johnson Oatman[71] that puts everything into perspective:

When you are discouraged, thinking all is lost,
Count your many blessings, name them one by one
…

Count your blessings, see what God hath done

Are you ever burdened with a load of care?
Does the cross seem heavy you are called to bear?
Count your many blessings, every doubt will fly,
And you will be singing as the days go by
…

So, amid the conflict, whether great or small,
Do not be discouraged, God is over all;
Count your many blessings, angels will attend,
Help and comfort give you to your journey's end.

Do Your Part

Start believing and give thanks for that dream that's been buried. Begin by simply telling your story just like we saw earlier with Giannis, in the movie *Rise,* who admitted that all he had to do was his part. When faced with self-doubt and other fears he used his and his family's story, their past, their survival, and he showed how that equipped him to stand out against other players.

Don't dwell on the negatives and bury your dream with "I can't"; "I will never get there". Get a shovel out to remove the dirt that's burying your dream and start throwing the positives that you have going for you no matter how small they may seem to you. Say thank you, Lord, for you promised me the desires of my heart. No matter how impossible it may seem, I know that I can do all things through Christ who strengthens me (Philippians 4:13). You may need to get some alone, quiet time with the Lord to get in agreement with him. Do your part to unearth that dream and bring it to life just like the trio of brothers who are now NBA stars in league history. You, too, are a star in your league, so go on, let your story shine!

In the book of Numbers, the Israelites had been living in the wilderness for forty years with God's guidance. Twelve spies were sent to assess Canaan, their promised land of milk and honey. All they had to do was their part, then leave the rest to the Lord. Ten of the spies came back with news of how the land was indeed prosperous with great fruit but mostly spread a negative report on how they would be up against much stronger people; they would be like grasshoppers in the face of the giants and did not have the ability to take over the land. They instilled fear in the rest of the people.

The other two spies, Joshua and Caleb, came back with a positive report, saying they would be able to take the land. They believed and had faith in the Lord who had guided, protected and provided for them for the past forty years in the wilderness. They urged the others to simply do their part by not being afraid, for God was with them and they would see a victory in the face of those stronger people.

The Israelites chose to go with the negative report of the other ten spies. They were afraid and, as a result, ended up back in the desert wandering for another forty years, with most of them dying there. They did not get to see the promised land, but Joshua and Caleb did.

As I read this story during my struggles (my giants) – the story of the ten spies and the rest of the Israelites became one of my greatest fears or lessons on **what not to do**. It stood as my biggest reminder whenever I faced challenges with my weighty excuses or a copious list of fears relating to which choice to make.

Do your part to stay positive, choose to be faithful not fearful and not die before you get to live your destiny, to reach your land of milk and honey.

Joshua and Caleb could have felt defeated and given up on the dream or felt other people caused their dream to get buried, but they chose to shell off the dirt with the positives.

Lori,[72] an ordinary person like you and me, shared her success story after the death of her husband and how she went from going into a negative space of wishing she, too, was with him to be happier and healthier than ever before. She attributes this to the help of her support network, which consisted of her family, support group, her church family, therapist, hospital, a radio station, music and above all, forming a relationship with God, reading her Bible to keep her going as she received the much-needed treatment. She still faces some rough times, but she says that she stands strong now and is unafraid to tell her story in the hope that it also impacts someone with whatever they might be going through.

From the story of Joshua and Caleb in biblical times to that of NBA basketball superstars and an ordinary person like Lori in our time, one thing stands out: the spirit God gave us is not of fear but that of power, love and sound mind (self-discipline, self-control) (2 Timothy 1:7).

As we face and conquer our giants, let's remember to do our part.

Walking Like Giants by Stars Go Dim is a thanks and praise song that strongly resonates with me: "His strength inside us, we're all fighters made to rise."

> ♪ **To listen to the song:**
> https://www.youtube.com/watch?v=Glent8xwAL4

Communing with God

All up it was three years of challenges for me from the time when the marriage issues started before the babymoon to the time I eventually moved into a new home as a single parent. In the waiting period before hitting that time, what I did know without a shadow of doubt is the spirit was doing its work and there would be a resurrection in God's right time. I had to just continue working on keeping the faith, holding on and waiting. I went backwards in the story to read about Jesus's last supper/Passover meal before his death.

I had a repeat message on breaking bread/communion. It originally came to me at a creative church conference I attended. I collected a couple of grape juice offerings that we had been encouraged to take with us for our personal or individual communion at home. (I found one of them in Tinotenda's pram a few weeks later, unopened – and very stale! So, I clearly didn't put it into practice until I got the message again.)

In 1 Corinthians 11, Paul said that he received the message from the Lord that when you break bread you are proclaiming Jesus's death until he comes again.

> "19 And he took bread, and when he had given thanks, he broke it and gave it to them, saying, 'This is my body, which is given for you. Do this in remembrance of me.' 20 And likewise the cup after they had eaten, saying, 'This cup that is poured out for you is the new covenant in my blood.'" (Luke 22:19-20 NIV)

Jesus did this with his disciples before facing his death on the cross: he gave thanks and shared communion with them confirming how by his grace, his death would save many lives, including mine. As I read that, I felt the urge to take communion on my own and stopped my reading there to reflect and listen more. I gave thanks to Jesus for his body given up and blood poured out for my impurities.

Recognise the wrong, ask for forgiveness, work on not committing the same sin and move on by being a better person from it.

I listened to some sermons on the blood and power of Jesus Christ. I understood that Catholics take communion at every mass because it means to abide in Jesus and for him to abide in you. Jesus is said to have given thanks despite knowing the betrayal that was coming with the crucifixion.

This is exactly what my spirit wanted me to take note of – how to give thanks and take communion. Pastor Bill Johnson encourages this[73] and highlights how it is not just a church ritual but something we can do on our own when facing difficulties. For me, it became clear that this is what I would do, just like taking prescribed medicine for whatever disease I was fighting. Take your communion, give thanks and pray over it for yourself, family, friends or whatever situation.

Breaking bread/communion is not meant to be a Sunday service ritual but something we do regularly, especially in our challenges until the Lord comes and breathes life into that dead situation or what appears dead. He has done it before and will do it again.

In communion, we are shouting God's death and salvation till he comes. We are engaging military effects over the situation in our lives. Delighting in Christ has an effect on those situations. Focus on him, his provision, the good not the evil, as it's said thankful people make breakthroughs.

Weapons of Warfare

We tend to ask or pray for the challenges to go away, but we learn that this has to be according to God's purpose. Jesus was the son of God in human form, and he called out to his Father ('Abba', which is the equivalent of 'daddy') to help by taking away the cup, the suffering from him only if it was his Father's will and not his own. He called out three times, showing how human and desperate he was.

In Mark 14, Jesus invited his support network, his disciples, to pray with him. Jesus took Peter, James and John. He acknowledged his distress and trouble. He even described how the sorrow that overwhelmed him was like death. Jesus chose to fight the battle he faced by leaning on his friends and surrendering in prayer to God's will for whom anything is possible.

Through Jesus's victory in facing death, defeating it as he rose again for the forgiveness of our failings, then leaving us his spirit as our guide and comforter, I have since learned of five weapons of warfare:

- **The name of God** – the name of our Father, the Son – Jesus Christ and the Holy Spirit

- **Communion** – the body and the blood of Jesus

- **The Word** – God's promises in the Bible

- **Thanks** and

- **Praise** – focusing on God's nature

I got the enlightenment that thanks and praise is expressing appreciation and understanding of God's nature and worth. His ways are higher than my ways; he rose from the dead to life and can do this for any situation in my life, according to his will. By saying thank you for each aspect of his divine nature our inward attitude becomes our outward expression. As we praise God, we expand our awareness of who he is.

In giving gratitude, we are encouraged to take note of God's attributes or characteristics in our readings and give thanks or praise for those. From Psalm 9, I found myself giving thanks and praise for all his wonderful deeds and his unshakeable loyalty in never forsaking those who seek him. It cemented my faith and trust in him as I began to note and see wonderful deeds that I might not have reflected on.

I came across a sermon by pastor Craig Groeschel[74] on giving praise to God with all you have (shigionoth) in the dark times like Habakkuk did. Habakkuk's name means wrestle and embrace. He was a prophet who wrestled with God due to the awful things happening to his people, but he also turned to embrace God. In this case, God responded to Habakkuk saying that he was going to help to save his people by bringing their worst enemies against them! Essentially, he was going to make the bad situation worse, so how could that be helping? Well, as I have described earlier, I have experienced times when he used seemingly worse situations for an unexpected outcome in my favour. Earlier in the book I discussed that praise is for **who he is** not for **what he does**.

Habakkuk's response was giving praise before provision with all he had:

"Though the fig tree does not bud and there are no grapes on the vines. Though the olive crop fails, and the fields produce no food, though there are no sheep in the pen, and no cattle in the stalls 18 yet I will rejoice in the Lord, I will be joyful in God my Savior. 19 The Sovereign Lord is my strength, he makes my feet like the feet of a deer, he enables me to tread on the heights." (Habakkuk 3:17-19 NIV)

From Habakkuk's story, we see that even if we complain to God, we learn:

1. Not to walk away from God

2. Not to quit on God but wait

3. Even if he doesn't change the circumstances, he will change our perspective – making our feet like deer to walk on the high places.

We may wrestle God but don't let go, embrace him. On the mountaintops praise him for what he has done. In the valleys, even if you go lower, praise him for **who he is,** so when you come back to the top you are like James, considering it pure joy in the valley. When it's finished you come out with perseverance, mature and complete – lacking nothing (James 1:2-4). It is just like the lyrics in 'Highlands (Song of Ascent)'[75]: "You're the summit where my feet are so I will praise You in the valleys all the same."

> ♫ **To listen to the song:**
> https://www.youtube.com/watch?v=JmskgTvTNq8

Rejoice

On my 30th day of journalling gratitude, I had a very fitting reading – Psalm 16:

> "9 Therefore my heart is glad, and my tongue rejoices; my body also will rest secure, 10 because you will not abandon me to the realm of the dead, nor will you let your faithful one see decay. 11 You make known to me the path of life; you will fill me with joy in your presence, with eternal pleasures at your right hand." (Psalm 16:9-11 NIV)

In both the good and not so good circumstances, there was reason to rejoice in God, who was my guide. He had not abandoned me, and despite feeling dead earlier on in my journey, he showed me the path to life.

On the third and final day of my monthly fast in this period, I got yet another timely message from the book of Joshua. Israel at this stage had spent yet another forty years in the desert since their escape from Egyptian slavery with Moses. Joshua was now their leader.

> "5 Joshua told the people, 'Consecrate yourselves, for tomorrow the Lord will do amazing things among you.' ... 7 the Lord said to Joshua, 'Today I will begin to exalt you in the eyes of all Israel, so they may know that I am with you as I was with Moses ...'" (Joshua 3:5-7 NIV)

The Jordan had been flooded during the harvest, but when the priests carrying an ark got to river, the water from upstream stopped flowing. (Joshua 3:15-16 NIV)

Joshua later spoke to the Israelites, telling them to pass on what had happened to their descendants.

> "22 tell them, 'Israel crossed the Jordan on dry ground.' 23 For the Lord your God dried up the Jordan before you until you had crossed over ... 24 He did this so that all the peoples of the earth might know that the hand of the Lord is powerful and so that you might always fear ['fear' as in feel profound awe and reverence] the Lord your God." (Joshua 4:22-24 NIV)

Israel's enemies were already afraid of them before they crossed the Jordan river. They had heard stories of how their God had protected them in the past by drying up the Red Sea for them to cross when they left Egypt. When they marched and blew trumpets with a loud shout around the Jericho walls as instructed by God, the walls came tumbling down, and they eventually won their promised land. (Joshua 6)

I read this as a message that as you purify yourself in prayer and rejoice in God, he will exalt you. With the Lord's favour you don't even have to sweat it, just stand and take your position and watch how much he will do for you when he moves. Praise God in that situation because that is a sure way out of that mess to the message.

As the saying goes,

> "God-ordained opportunities are brilliantly disguised as problems and challenges."

> "Nothing is impossible, the word itself says 'I'm possible!'"

Audrey Hepburn

Motivational speaker Eddie Pinero describes one of his favourite songs, the world-famous hit 'Iris' by Goo Goo Dolls, which was crafted from a seemingly impossible situation. The band's frontman, singer-songwriter John Rzeznik's life was in a shambles. He was coming out of a divorce, a bad record deal with a label had kept most of his revenue, he had writer's block, felt like a phoney and was living in a hotel.

His manager called him to tell him of an opportunity that had come up to work on the soundtrack for the 1998 movie *City of Angels* with Meg Ryan and Nicolas Cage. He auditioned for it with only two lines and a guitar with two broken strings. Basically, all odds seemed stacked against him, but he rocked up, nevertheless. This was the origin of the song 'Iris', a big hit and one of the most well-known Goo Goo Dolls songs. It's a demonstration of how seemingly impossible situations can disguise great opportunities.

By sharing the message in his mess, John Rzeznik brought a source of healing, hope and whatever else, not just for himself but millions of others all over the world.

> ♫ **To listen to the song:**
> https://www.youtube.com/watch?v=NdYWuo9OFAw

"Rejoice in the Lord always (no matter the circumstances); again I will say rejoice." (Philippians 4 ESV).

Praise and worship songs I listened to in rejoicing:

'Ridza Bhosvo':[76] The literal translation of the Shona song title is 'blow your trumpet'.

It is inspired by the story in Joshua 6 – when the Israelites went around the walls praising and rejoicing at the Fall of Jericho. The song is about giving praise – *masvingo enhamo dzako dzese,* meaning blow your trumpet around the walls/fort of all your problems and praise the God of miracles. Rejoice over your problems no matter what, even seemingly insurmountable ones like Israel versus Jericho, David versus Goliath, Samson versus the Philistines and Daniel in the lion's den.

> ♫ **To listen to the song:**
> https://youtu.be/hvRPQk8uWts

'Malibongwe igama lakho':[77] The translation of the Zulu (South African) is 'Let Your Name Be Praised'.

'Kulungile Baba':[78] It's Okay/All Is Well, Papa/Dad.

> ♫ **To listen to the song:**
> https://www.youtube.com/watch?v=Ddz7IkOIOFk

Put a Smile on and Sing His Praise

One of my girlfriends who checked in on me frequently to give me spiritual support once said, "Remember, at times you agree with God on what you want to be the result, just not on how to get there. He is in charge of the *how*; you are responsible for keeping the faith, praising and giving thanks no matter what comes."

Joy at times doesn't come to us automatically and we need to stir ourselves up to fight the good fight of faith: we have to say "God, I want to put a smile on my face and am going to sing a song of praise even though I don't see anything happening." A song that inspires me in this vein is 'Grace to Grace':

"And from death to life, I will sing Your praise
In the wonder of Your grace".[79]

> ♪ **To listen to the song:**
> https://www.youtube.com/watch?v=lPdGOdubic8

Psalm 100 A Psalm for Giving Grateful Praise

"4 Enter his gates with thanksgiving and his courts with praise; give thanks to him and praise his name. 5 For the Lord is good and his love endures forever; his faithfulness continues through all generations." (Psalms 100:4-5 NIV)

TAKEAWAYS

- Remember that thanks and praise is how we fight our battles.

- Be thankful even for your trials and tribulations – they are valuable lessons learned.

- Be glad – enjoying life depends on the attitude you have towards it.

- Don't ask 'why' something happened. Instead, ask what you can learn from it and give thanks for the 'what'.

- Give thanks even when you have a heavy heart.

- Move your focus away from fault-finding.

- Learn to focus on what you have to be grateful for by eliminating distractions (for example, social media).

- Keep a gratitude journal and list even the smallest things you are thankful for.

PART 4

Seasons

WINTER IS JUST A SEASON

SEASONS – **Winter**, Spring, Summer, Autumn (Fall)

WINTER is **just but a season**, it **will pass** – all is well.

Instagram Photographer - bartezzz82

"There is a time for everything, and a season
for every activity under the heavens."

(Ecclesiastes 3:1 NIV)

Instagram Photographer - spring, summer, autumn - bartezzz82

WINTER IS JUST A SEASON

When all is said and done, we must understand that in our personal lives we will experience different times and seasons without fail, just like in nature. There is a time for everything and so we need to understand the season we are in to know how to utilise it wisely for the greatest reward. Author Jim Rohn used the 'parable of the sower' to give insight into how our lives are affected by the different seasons.

As you go through the winter of life facing different challenges, be it personal or financial difficulties, remember the season will change to move on to the next, so don't judge your life based on your winter or whatever season you are in, but do find the purpose in it and learn from it.[80]

I have also realised that from year to year, it will not always be a bed of roses or basking in the sun in spring or summer, even if I have just had a tough winter.

With a better understanding of the seasons in my life, I have become more equipped to keep working on myself.

Author and master yoga teacher Ram Jain discusses the point that there are seasons in our personal lives, just like in nature:[81]

WINTER – sadness, heartbreak, loneliness, sickness

I could relate to the winter aspects – winter was the whole mess in my life – the great difficulties during my marital challenges, mourning plus solo, first-time parenting. It turned out to be a time to sharpen tools just as a farmer would, to learn and prepare to follow the plan of action. During that same period, I identified the message in it as well, to keep going and eventually share my story with the world.

SPRING – hope, new beginnings, opportunities

With the eventual sale of the matrimonial house, it was like the light at the end of the tunnel. There was definite hope, new beginnings, opportunities as it tied into the move and purchase of the new home as a single parent, plus all court proceedings settling. Our new home was well located for the transition and our needs.

SUMMER – signs of growth, need for protection, an abundance of distractions

With the lessons learned in the winter and the hope from spring there was definite growth to be shared with others for their own walk.

I did struggle with how to best extract that message out of my mess – all my journalling put together forming about 700+ pages. I also saw the need for protection as I didn't want to relive what I had been through in compiling this book. I wanted the ultimate message of hope to come across considering all the relationships involved. I couldn't budge from there or had writer's block and sat on the consolidated journals for about a year. I started to date again forming new relationships, went away on holidays with my girl, friends and family.

All in all, I had enough distractions, and, in a way, it did feel like a well-deserved much-needed summer holiday. On the flip side, I also realised that the welcome distractions could hinder progress on the writing project if left unmanaged, so I eventually got back on track with that. I also encountered some hindrances out of my control that were distracting my progress. It started to feel like winter again if I didn't persevere to the end goal of publishing my story. I had to choose to learn from the past and use tools to protect my growth and achievements. I needed to live in the moment and redirect my focus towards my goals.

FALL (AUTUMN) – successes and achievements, failures

With this season, after effort and patience, we harvest what was planted.

Ram Jain encourages us to accept and take responsibility for our harvest-time results. Celebrate the success and reflect on the failures to see what it is we missed and how we can do better.

All in all, he highlights how seasons are not in our control, but our actions are. We cannot change the seasons, but we can change ourselves.

Thriving in Adversity

I found the song 'Seasons' so jam-packed with hope in my winter. It lifted my spirit as I sang it, knowing that the colder the winter, the more I had to dig my heels in for there was plenty for me to learn before I could reap the fruit from that harvest. It was only when I had worked my way through many trials, and I was ready for a fresh start, that I came to fully understand the song:[82]

"For Your promise is loyal
From seed to sequoia".

Though the winter is long, it will lead to a giant harvest like a sequoia. The writer likens this to the birth of Christ, who came to us as a baby and had to wait until adulthood to fulfil the promise that he was born for by dying on the cross to save us. Even Jesus's rising was on the third day. God as God could have done this whole saving process in a second, but he didn't. He took his time to go through the seasons until all the work he wanted done was finished. There is a time for everything.

> ♫ **To listen to the song:**
> https://www.youtube.com/watch?v=G5TgsPI_IU0

I was intrigued when Ben Hastings, one of the 'Seasons' songwriters, gave some insight into the line in the song 'from seed to sequoia'.[83] He discussed how from a small pinhead sequoia seed grows the largest tree in the world. Ninety-one thousand seeds add up to a single pound / 0.45 kilograms, with the largest of the sequoias as tall as a 26-storey building. From such a small ordinary seed grows something extraordinary, and it is the winter harshness that makes the tree grow strong and allows it to thrive to its fullness and everything it is meant to be.

> "As regards some of the trees, I want them preserved because they are the only things of their kind in the world. Lying out at night under those giant Sequoias was lying in a temple built by no hand of man, a temple grander than any human architect could by any possibility

build, and I hope for the preservation of the groves of giant trees simply because it would be a shame to our civilization to let them disappear. They are monuments in themselves ..."[84]

Theodore Roosevelt, 1903 speech in Sacramento, California

Sequoias also depend on forest fires to regenerate. Giant sequoias can not only survive forest fires, but they thrive on them. The seeds inside the cones on the forest floor are released by heat that opens them up. Deadwood is turned to nutrient-rich ash which is perfect for the seeds' successful growth. Before forest rangers were aware of the benefits of fire for renewing, they would extinguish the fire then wonder why there was no new growth. The rangers now intentionally set controlled fire to simulate the natural regeneration process.[85]

The word 'regenerate' is from Latin regeneratus 'created again', past participle of regenerare, from re- 'again' + generare 'create'.[86]

It is interesting to note that the harsh winter is key to growing strong, and fire is necessary for new growth, with what is considered dead being used as nutrients. This is important for us to apply in our lives as we go through our winters. As our life is in the fiery furnace, we need to remember that, though at times we might feel like death, we are not dead. It is a growth process toward becoming an improved version of ourselves.

There are those who have mastered the harshness of winter or being under fire and have grown to be giants in this world like sequoia trees. In the movie *Chang Can Dunk*, Kobe Bryant, one of the greatest basketball players and scorers of all time, is said to have looked at:

obstacles = opportunities

every challenge = chance for improvement

The million-dollar question is: What about you? What are the opportunities in your obstacles?

Watching the movie as Chang talked about his hero Kobe made me feel invincible, but it also woke me up to pay attention to how I processed problems or applied that perspective in my life.

The marital challenges were now over. I was learning to walk as a single parent. In the week I watched the film, I unexpectedly got a string of attacks health-wise and financially, so I was very challenged by this question in real time. There was one thing after another to test me, just as I had celebrated some big wins before.

It had been over a couple of years since the purchase of a new home that suited my girl and me well in terms of keeping her in the same day care area, considering all the other changes she had already been through. It also opened better government school opportunities, which put my mind at ease, knowing I had options to help me balance things financially depending on how I went with everything in a single-parent household. The previous location fell within the catchment of some of the best schools for primary school, but the new location also now meant we qualified to apply in the high school zone too.

It was as if since the move into the new house I had spring, filled with new beginnings and opportunities. I had planted different seeds through my various projects.

As I finalised my writing in 2023, based on my past experiences, it was as if I was being retested and back in winter again. I had just finished paying off a credit card that had been long outstanding, but suddenly, all that work seemed to unravel as I racked up bills in the thousands over a week. With the interest rate hikes and looking to refinance my home loan it seemed I was taking steps backwards to work on improving my borrowing capacity.

My expenses included a major dental bill and an MRI for pain in my hands that couldn't be worked out from blood tests or X-rays. I had to type for a living at work and to finish my writing project, but each morning I was waking up with excruciating pain in my hands. As I was working on getting my head around it all, I also had a wardrobe door in my five-year-old's bedroom fall and shatter tiny glass pieces from her mirror all over the carpet. Thank God that she wasn't hurt – it could have been worse. I had her settled in the other room then went on to vacuum the carpet and as Murphy's law would have it, the vacuum cleaner also then died. I decided to let it go and aim for joy in the new day.

I researched the best tradie bill to add getting the mirror fixed to my to-do list. A few days later, my two-year-old phone with zero cracks (because I had learned my lesson from the past and put the strongest screen and phone protector I could find) also decided to just freeze up on me, then go kaput. The phone repairers could not go past the logo sign after a forced restart and couldn't fix it. Just what I needed. But it could only look up from there! Well, that's what I thought.

A few minutes after picking my daughter up from school, the car dashboard flashed a sign 'overheating engine temperature, please stop safely'. I was first in line at a traffic light when the car just came to a halt. I didn't quite know what it meant and was confused because the car had been for service literally two months earlier, and I had paid good money for it. As I sat there hitting the hazard button, I thought I could feel my feet burning, but the confusion had me muddled up and not quite sure. The car started again, and I just parked it a few metres away from the traffic on the side of the road, then quickly got out of the car with my daughter.

As we stood outside, my daughter noticed what we thought at the time was smoke at the driver's seat, but I was later advised it was steam from the heater cooler in the dashboard, which explained the burning sensation I felt on my legs. At the time, though, I thought the 'smoke' meant our car could have blown up whilst we were driving. It was the last straw for me. I took a moment of silence and put my head in my lap for a bit of a somewhat private cry. I certainly couldn't remember when I last had the waterworks. I'd had a very good run. I wondered what was going on. Literally, one thing after the other was going wrong. I thought of Kobe Bryant's way of life again and his legacy that lives on, even though he is not physically with us anymore. I kept asking myself – What is the opportunity in my obstacle – the chance of improvement in my challenge?

At first glance it certainly felt like a trick question – thanks, Kobe! I had a quick check in with myself as I gathered my thoughts about my morning reading that day to help me find comfort.

"1 Have mercy on me, my God, ... I will take refuge in the shadow of your wings until the disaster has passed. 2 I cry out to God Most High ... 3 He sends from heaven and saves me, ... God sends forth his love and his faithfulness." (Psalms 57:1-3 NIV)

Literally, the words from my random Bible reading that morning were heaven sent. Taking refuge in the shadow of his wings and sending forth love and faithfulness were the words that were drawn to my spirit as I recalled past lessons that had given me strength. I was gently reminded how the darkness is a shadow of his wings protecting me as per the song and song-story 'Surrounded (Fight My Battles' (discussed earlier), and in Lamentations 3 – his love endures forever as great is his faithfulness.

As I had my little moment, I had switched off the engine and was now sitting with my daughter in safety by the side of the road. My head hiding in my lap, half crying, half reciting the words in prayer to myself – no doubt I looked like a crazy person! A lady and her husband stopped their car to come check on us. At that stage, I had a hundred million thoughts running through my head but hadn't really stopped to fully appreciate how fortunate we had been to get out on time and save not only ourselves but any other cars or pedestrians from danger. The strangers who stopped to see how we were reminded me of God sending his love and being faithful. I was grateful to them, our angels on Earth and for the goodness I knew was in the chaos.

Even though it might have seemed like something was out to get me with a string of bad events, with each challenge there was either a stranger, colleague, friend, family member or neighbour who sought to help us out from the goodness of their heart, reiterating the love sent forth for me. On that day it so happened a friend was in the vicinity and came to pick us up. Her sister had a warm meal ready for dinner for us. Neighbours and friends offered their car for us to drive. A tow truck driver ended up taking the car to the service garage that same day.

The car was taken to those who had serviced it just two months earlier; I expected that they would have picked the issue up. They advised their checks and tests at service time had not revealed any problems. The issue was with the heater core system that is hidden behind the dashboard. They referred me to the car manufacturer dealership as the issue was too major for them to address. After about three mechanic visits and more bills, the problem finally got resolved.

I was challenged to seek opportunities and find ways to improve during my health and financial challenges. I went through self-development and discovered some life lessons. I was also reminded that fire might be needed to kill off stagnation. Rather than being back in winter as I had initially thought, I was in summer, going through a growth phase. My plans had stagnated a little, especially the writing project. I had to dig deep to find ways to protect the work I had done so far and continue to nourish it to fruition, even with all the changes. I had the powerful advantage of having acquired strength from the past harsh winter.

Following a similar train of thought on obstacles = opportunities and every challenge = a chance for improvement, there was also an interesting story shared by Alexandra Eldens (CEO and founder of Big Life Journal)[87]. When she was in grad school, she went to offload her problems to Fred, her counsellor. She was going through one of those rough patches with her finance studies lagging behind, a car accident where she hit a pole, an out-of-control roommate's cat and the list went on, just like mine seemed to during my problem-packed season. When she was done venting, Fred calmly pointed out, "Sounds like you've got some interesting projects there", which puzzled Alexandra. Her counsellor then elaborated on how problems = projects. By starting to see the problems that way, it gave her a different perspective.

This difference in thinking is empowering. Big Life Journal talks about how our mindset impacts our life and taking small actions that ultimately add up leads to making a big change. It starts with how we think > changing how we feel > which changes how we act > which impacts the life we have. For Alexandra, instead of dwelling on her mountain of problems, she found herself thinking of different projects to tackle. She now had a finance studies project and worked on organising a better study schedule. She researched the behaviour of cats and found ways for the cat to be less aggressive. Instead of problem-focus with a negative mentality spiralling into complaining and self-pity parties, the new perspective brings about solution-focus with positive thinking.

A Chance in the World

Steve Pemberton[88] was an orphan who landed in an abusive foster family and was labelled as not having 'a chance in the world' by a babysitter who handed him over to the foster system. In the face of adversity, he ultimately ended up finding love, hope and a home. People often fail to see that challenges are a pathway to exploration and discovery. It's either you lament and languish or believe and build; Steve chose the latter. He survived childhood abuse through people he saw as human lighthouses. They were a light in his life, like his neighbour who gave him books, his teacher, social worker and others who were there for him in different ways. They listened, encouraged him or simply gave him a smile that got him to face or survive one more day, probably without them even realising the impact on his life. He was empowered to also be a light for someone else so that they, in turn, could be a light for another and so on.

There is a saying that necessity is the mother of invention, but Steve thinks it's adversity. The middle step between adversity, exploration and discovery to get to his final step of vision and solution was education. Books gave him the power to overcome adversity. I believe it was the same for me with books and people's stories in whatever shape. Be it the stories from ancient times in the Bible or from the current times through day-to-day encounters in person or online, novels, testimonies, movies and songs, I found a nugget of something to help me face one day, then another, and now years have gone by in that manner.

I have learned that I am better in a one-on-one chat. Interestingly, this explains why, at my surprise baby shower (the best surprise to date for me, considering I had said that I didn't want to have one nor did I expect people to fuss), I ended up with a house full of people. In a group scenario, I am a little bit of a fish out of water, but the one-on-one relationships I am better at all add up to form a decent-sized group. That same group of people, through their love, turned out to be my support network in the tough times, to lift me up so that I could be a human lighthouse for others.

Out-of-Body Experiences

What I learned in earlier years could sustain me through any other cycle to come, including the one in 2023. I believe my out-of-body experiences in 2018 played a part in facing what appeared to be insurmountable during my tough season.

Mindvalley, hosted by Vishen Lakhiani, looked at something similar from a neuroscience perspective with regard to extraordinary performance through Steven Kotler's story.[89] They discussed how a lot of what leads us to achieve peak performance has much more to do with the state of consciousness than our skill sets. They refer to the habit of ferocity. The world's best entrepreneurs, artists, athletes and visionaries harness ferocity to achieve seemingly impossible feats. Passion and perseverance are needed but are not sufficient to get us through. Steven Kotler interviewed celebrities who made it and found that many went through real challenges.

A lot of us are hardwired for mediocrity being creatures of habit and fear, but we all want a meaningful life. We are faced with one challenge after the other, pushing a little harder, believing when we get to a certain stage then it's going to get easy – when I get this job, car, married, house and so on. This was true for me. I thought after I had passed through the harshest of winters, then it was going to generally be easy peasy lemon squeezy from then on, almost like life owed me a bit of a break and whatever difficulties would be cruisy. When I then found each win almost getting tallied up with another challenge, it seemed a bit out of whack.

Lead performers seem to rise to a challenge effortlessly before they even realise they are doing so. They get through several life problems in a day without stopping. If they did stop, then fear of it being difficult would cripple them, so they wouldn't get where they want to go. I found this is when procrastination kicks in for me, and I have been encouraged to just start by breaking it down into smaller steps to action instead, then go from there.

WINTER IS JUST A SEASON

When hard times ramp up, the habit of ferocity is to take them and turn them into challenges. Don't be like I was at the start of my journey, curling up into a ball of fear and continuous sadness from days to weeks to months on end, then driving myself into depression. With a change in habits and the default setting, as Steven Kotler says, you can be halfway through a challenge before even realising you are.

Steven's experience came from his battle with Lyme disease (which comes from the bites of ticks) when he was thirty years old. He spent most of three years in bed. He went bankrupt seeking a cure, lost the woman that he was going to marry and a job he had spent a decade getting. The effects on him were physically debilitating – he couldn't walk across a room, and he was losing his memory, including short-term and hallucinating. Doctors had no idea if he would make it and pulled him off medication because his stomach lining was bleeding out as a reaction to the antibiotics.

Steven now saw himself only as a burden on his family and friends. He contemplated killing himself, deciding it was not *if* but *when*. Before he got to that, a friend of his visited and insisted on taking him surfing, even though he wasn't very good at it. He could hardly walk across a room, but she kept badgering and would not leave his house. Two people helped him to the car and to a beach in Los Angeles.

When he got to surfing, he had an out-of-body experience, which was like he had a panoramic vision and was hovering above his body. He felt alive and saw possibilities. He caught about five waves that day, and when he got back home, he was so sick that he couldn't walk for fourteen days. On the fifteenth day when he could, he managed to convince a neighbour to take him surfing again.

He describes the out-of-body experience as the flow state and says it brought him healing.

For Steven, doing the impossible is about constantly training yourself to be your best at your worst. Find your compass to keep going in the right direction and magnify your productivity towards your dreams.

My out-of-body experiences were different, but they served as a point of reference for me to keep going and rooting myself in who God is and his promises, especially when challenged. The first encounter was when I was in the thick of it with the separation and divorce issues. I sang 'Surrounded (Fight My Battles)' (mentioned earlier) repeatedly one beautiful sunny day with my little girl playing at my side. I found great comfort and complete rest in the song; that is when I had my aha moment or revelation that thanks and praise is how I fight my battles, and that even though I was surrounded by problems, I was also surrounded by God.

As I sang my heart out on this particular day in the lounge room of our matrimonial home, I felt an unmistakable spirit come to surround me. It all happened in a flash, but it was as though someone came and draped a white garment on me – like a garment of praise – the anointing of the Spirit was upon me! (My promise – Isaiah 61). I was convinced beyond the shadow of a doubt that each word in Isaiah 61 was for me and took it as a reminder to keep on going each time challenges ramp up.

This out-of-body experience, which was something new for me, reminded me of a few times my mother shared stories of certain people's out-of-this-world experiences and the impact on their lives. I recall that I only really half-listened to these, secretly thinking 'As if!'. However, it was an entirely different thing after I had my own mind-blowing encounter and learned to use it to fuel my life when I was in a hopeless state.

A few months down the track that same year, I felt that strong presence of God again. This time, it was deep in the night as I scrolled through some complimentary eBook offers that I had got from the Bevere bookstore. I had to make a selection, and I wanted to take advantage of this offer to pick the best options for the season I was in. Something prompted me to stop and first listen to a prayer I had received. It was from someone who didn't even know my story at a church conference during a spirit-moving prayer session. People who felt the spirit lead them to pray over someone were encouraged to take the courage to ask the person to do so. I had nothing in that session, but I was open to it and stayed in my position as I prayed on my own.

One girl came over and asked to pray over me. I just listened, very interested to hear what it was she had to say. She saw my heart for women and children. She could see me surrounded by them and then also saw a man in a lion skin standing behind me. I was a little taken aback because in my private time at home I had written down in my journal my desire to do charity work with a focus on women and children. I had talked about it with a handful of my close friends in the comfort of our home. She would have had no idea about it, although it meant I could relate to the first part of her prayer.

For the longest time, I questioned the other part – who the man in the lion skin was. Being the typical human that I am, led by flesh, at some stage I took it to possibly be my future man, a partner who would work with me in God's work and purpose for life. It took me until that moment deep in the night to realise without a doubt that man was actually Jesus and not an earthly man as I had originally thought. It was glaringly obvious then, and I couldn't even see how I missed it for so long. I then went ahead to listen to the eBook options I had. When I got to the *Lioness Arising* book by Lisa Bevere,[90] there was a chapter that I sampled that tied everything together for me.

As I walked towards the walk-in wardrobe in my bedroom, there was an undeniable presence with me every step that I took. When I was right by the door, I felt a strong and loud confirmation in my spirit: "I will never leave you nor forsake you and I am the lion of Judah." It made my hair stand on end as I got a deeper meaning of fear of the Lord with that experience, and I was in awe of it all. The eBook I ended up picking, *Lioness Arising*, encourages us to change our world through that vision and purpose in life that we have, which aligned with exactly what I already had in my journal and where my head space was at. To say that it was mind-blowing is an understatement.

The following year, in 2019, I had another encounter at church. Sanga shared his message that Sunday morning from Luke 4, a reading by Jesus after he had faced multiple tests in the wilderness during his fast and before people from his hometown of Nazareth rejected him. Jesus read from the scroll (book) of Isaiah:

"18 The Spirit of the Lord is upon me,
because he has anointed me
to proclaim good news to the poor.
He has sent me to proclaim liberty to the captives
and recovering of sight to the blind,
to set at liberty those who are oppressed,
19 to proclaim the year of the Lord's favor." (Luke 4:18-19 ESV)

This was a repeat of the message I had drawn from the book of Isaiah 61 when I got my first encounter and promise in the living room the previous year. After Jesus talked about the scripture being fulfilled in their hearing, people tried to kill him. It is said that he walked through the crowd and went on his way to the next place and continued with his work.

Sanga encouraged us not to let our past kill us. You might have to walk through your past negatives, but God doesn't intend on having you stay there, so choose to keep walking. Get up and go on your way, don't stay in bitterness, revenge, unforgiveness, loss, hurt, depression, pain or failure. Don't live or camp there. The journey might take longer but keep walking through it until you are out.

At that time – during that second year of selling the house and still failing, which brought with it more challenges – my struggles just seemed to have no end. As the teaching came to a close, I felt like an actual physical presence of Christ himself comfort me in my seat and say, "It is over; it is finished". It was so unreal; I just broke down in tears saying, "Thank you!" I was more than convinced that faith for the promise is in the promise and you have to know what your promise is. Without a shadow of a doubt, that Word and teaching was for me.

That same week, one of my closest friends, who had no idea about my church service encounter, told me what had happened at a business award conference. She got talking to a pastor, Shone, and ended up referring to my challenges. As they were talking, the pastor shared that there was a sense of breakthrough and not to doubt that God was bringing me into a new season. I found it interesting since it seemed to align with my personal experience at church. All this happened before one potential buyer fell through soon after (which of course didn't make much sense in the physical in terms of the spiritual confirmation I'd had).

I have since learned that at times a confusing or opposite event is what's necessary to get you to the finish line. It's just like when we do something physically difficult. Just as we are about to get to the top or end of that challenge, our body seems to want to give up on us.

A couple of months from then the finalisation of an actual written contract for the sale of the house came through and brought my springtime. Finally, winter was over. It was finished! Faith and hope are a big part of what kept me walking to get me to the finish line.

With faith like a mustard seed you can say to a mountain move, and it will move. (Matthew 17:20)

Sanga from my church encourages us to stop talking about our mountain to everyone and start talking about our mountain with God. Don't look at the size of your seed. Faith comes from hearing the word of God again and again. The challenge is: will you keep walking even when it's not working? Will you keep your eyes fixed on him and his Word to see the season through? Faith makes you step out, one step at a time, one day at a time. God uses hurdles to rise; he uses crucifixion for resurrection. Just as he did with Jesus. It's what you do with the mountains, hurdles, and crucifixion in your life that's important.

I chose to put my faith in the divine power of the holy trinity – the Father, Son and Holy Spirit. That is bigger than the mountain, even with faith as little as a mustard seed. With this I got God's peace and stayed in balance despite my world falling apart. With the transition to the new home on my own with my girl and the new season in 2023, these out-of-body encounters stood out as a memorial to look back on what to do or work on.

A New Way to See Life and Overcome Challenges

Peak performers practise being their best at their worst. Steven Kotler has shared how he flies all over the world to give speeches in high-pressure meetings when he is jetlagged, tired and hasn't had a good sleep or a proper meal, with maybe a thousand other things that have gone wrong, but still has only one shot at nailing his content. It's all about facing fear, knowing that you can perform your best even at your worst and rising to the occasion.

The training that extreme athletes do involves staying in balance even when exhausted.

For physical training, Steven goes to the gym and does his normal workouts with some intensity sprints. He does the running machine and jumping rope, then goes on a balancing board holding a dumbbell for ten minutes without it touching the ground.

Personally, to stay in balance mentally and spiritually, meditation on the Word is a start for me, even if it means playing guided meditation from YouTube, YouVersion Bible or whatever app. At times, after reading, I simply take some quiet time or journal my thoughts on my own.

I have developed an enhanced understanding of the connection between my body, mind and soul (spirit). To be well-balanced and healthy overall, I now clearly see that just as I eat to feed my body, I have to fast to feed my spirit. I discovered I also have to run or exercise not only for my physical health but to feed my mind. For my mental and physical health, I have taken a baby-step approach with my gym sessions, and I have found it is also good training when dealing with my other projects.

I started off with 30:04+ then 45:04+ minute runs three times a week. During the runs, when I reach a point of difficulty, I learned the best way for me to get through to the end is by breaking it down into five-minute intervals. In my head, as I run, I aim for that small chunk of five minutes instead of 30 or 45+ minutes.

At times all I can do is walk to the gym and stand on the treadmill, then just keep holding on, simply taking one jog at a time until I get to the end of the session. In the Brisbane blazing heat, my gym is like a sauna and only has one giant fan that I move as close as possible to the treadmill. I feel I have every reason to quit – it's too hot (though in winter there are some days I tell myself it's cold even though it's the Sunshine state of Australia, lol!). As I run, especially in the middle or towards the end, I really just want to press the stop button and walk out because I feel I can't breathe, am going to die, my mind or legs just aren't up for it or whatever reasons my head comes up with. I have to fight a big mental battle, but one thing I tell myself as I walk to the gym, and even when I am there, is that I am not quitting today.

Sometimes I might break the runs down even further to aim to complete the first half of the five-minute intervals. I look forward to little treats, such as finishing the first ten minutes so I can wipe myself and have a sip of water as I run. My challenge for that day, in that moment, is simply to keep holding on till I finish what I started.

I later found this holding-on, breaking-down mentality helps with maintaining focus and achieving not just the project at hand but others, too, be it my book writing or whatever else when I feel overwhelmed.

After the run, I then do my push-ups. I switched that up to doing 3x30 second planks instead, then later increased that to 3x1:04+ minute planks to help me keep holding on further and practise staying in balance when I am exhausted. As the days go by, especially on hot days, I find it's still a hard exercise, but it's easier to handle based on how I decide to see, process, and overcome the challenge. On cooler days, the exercises are more enjoyable, but whatever the season, after I finish, I feel much better within myself – my mind is clearer and my spirit lighter. I am physically fitter, too, and all the excuses, like feeling I will die in the heat, disappear as it all translates to my other project work. (Note: This is how I do things; you should seek advice from health professionals for your own physical exercises.)

The athletes' extreme training is said to be similar to the fight or flight response. When faced with acute fear we fight, flee or freeze. These same conditions apply when we are anxious, and the more anxious we become, our options shrink.

When our life is at its worst, be it health-wise, due to complicated relationships at home, work, business or whatever it is, we need to train ourselves to be our best. Will you look at the tools you have at hand now and choose to fight, flee or freeze? The last two tend to be the natural or easier options to fall back on for me and probably others like me. As the Navy Seals saying goes, when you face a challenge: "you don't rise to the occasion, you sink to the level of your training. That's why we train so hard". The presence of fear limits our options, and so you get what you train for. Train to be your best when life keeps throwing challenges at you to help you automate 'rising to the occasion'.

In 2023, after reflection on my journey, I decided to do my planks after the runs when I am exhausted. I also added an extra 4+ seconds or minutes at times to my runs and planks as I aim to push just a little harder with them as a reminder to myself that in my life projects, I must rise to the level of how I train.

In all my projects, I say out loud to myself or take a mental note – "Remember, you rise to the level of your training" to help me keep going.

Everything Has Changed but Nothing Has Changed

At times, we get caught up in "if I could get this, that or the other", then I will be in a certain position. We eventually get there and find out nothing has changed. For example, we finally get married and realise everything has changed in getting married, but nothing has changed in terms of day-to-day living – we still need to cook, eat, pay bills and the like. Just as I eventually moved from the matrimonial house into one of my own and everything had drastically changed, but I still faced a set of responsibilities and challenges to get through, armed with armour from my past wins.

Parents-to-be shared at a church service how they found out that they were both healthy carriers of a gene that causes cystic fibrosis (CF) in kids. They talked to some close people, one of whom was a biologist. They realised that if they had known the statistics of what could go wrong from conception to birth, then they would not even have mated, which made them realise that everything had changed, but nothing had changed in God. Just as we faced different challenges in the pandemic, and now with the high cost of living, God has remained a God who can calm the storm or the wind. It is just a matter of maintaining our position of unwavering faith in him in the storm and the winds of life. (Matthew 8 and 14)

Use the Word to Overcome the World

In a faith series at a church service, Sloan shared that he doesn't respond well to unexpected events. Things happen in life that are out of our control. However, in school we are taught how to make money but not how to respond when, say, you lose all of it or when life happens, and we face certain losses.

In as much as we might not be in control of what happens, we can control our response. The Word teaches us how to respond.

The book of Psalms shows us how to do life with God and relate to God in our daily life when all is falling apart. Two main pillars that frame the Psalms:

Psalms 1 and 150

How to respond to everything that life throws at us:

1. Psalm 1 – Delight in the law of the Lord

Obedience is the proper way to respond to life and step out in our life. Get in the word of God and read it because it will never do you wrong as long as you make the decision to obey. To see what God would do about a situation, read the Word. It has the answers if you choose to read it and apply it. Through this, you will get to know God.

2. Psalm 150 – Praise the Lord

Psalms start with obedience and end with praise. We are encouraged to live a life of obedience and praise all the time. In the good and bad times when nothing makes sense, you will see his goodness, mercy, kindness and give him praise for his faithfulness in his love and in your midnight hour.

Romans 12 – praise like Paul in full view of God's mercy.

Open your eyes and see that God has been good, merciful, and so give him praise because he deserves all of it for giving his life up for us. At times, we don't see this because we are looking the other way. We need to turn to see the goodness of the Lord and see the cross and the power in the resurrection.

Psalms 73:1-5 – almost missing the Lord's goodness because of facing the other way and looking at other people.

If you decide to step out in faith and let go of everything to praise and thank him, then he will come and take over your life. Have an attitude of gratitude! What is taking up the real estate of your mind? Do you live in delight or duty?

Duty or Delight?

A teaching on how we choose to live our life out of duty or delight no matter the season was shared by Andy at a church service. There are certain seasons we go through that are hard to delight in. We should make the decision to live our life in delight no matter what.

At times, what was once a delight can turn into a duty.

Trust in the Lord, delight in the Lord, and he shall bring it to pass. (Psalms 37 NIV)

In the Sermon on the Mount, Jesus says,

> "You have heard that it was said, 'Eye for eye, and tooth for tooth.' But I tell you, do not resist an evil person. If anyone slaps you on the right cheek, turn to them the other cheek also … If anyone forces you to go one mile, go with them two miles." (Matthew 5:38-41 NIV)

Jesus introduced us to the one-mile rule: Roman soldiers could force Jewish people to drop whatever they were doing to carry their backpack for one mile and if someone refused to, they would be flogged. This forced the

Jews to hate the Romans, gentiles who ruled over them in their own country. Imagine then doing another mile when not asked! If you do it out of duty, you will find yourself doing it in the negative as you feel compelled to do it, and you will likely complain. Whereas when you do it out of delight, it comes from your heart and there are positives. It will be as per Psalm 37, if you delight in things of God, you will find joy in every season.

Imagine what would happen in the extra mile taken by the Jews? Roman soldiers would probably question why they bother doing the second mile, especially as they do it with delight. It is the second mile that triggers the conversation. Look at the different areas in your life and your response. Duty will have excuses – someone can do a better job, not my part, no time, money or energy. Delight says my contribution can bring joy to those around me: I will be the hands and feet of Christ or that angel for others here on Earth.

> "… whatever you did for one of the least of these brothers and sisters of mine, you did for me." (Matthew 25:40 NIV)

Andy told a story of a non-Christian gym owner in Brisbane who decided to promote a church doing a kilo Christmas bag for people in need. To get extra points towards gym membership, he encouraged the members to bring in a bag to help raise resources for their community and be a part of those who bring joy to others. Each person turned out to be an angel for people in need that Christmas.

I understood earlier on in my journey that my learning or teaching should be rooted in the Spirit of God in me and for his glory.

Breaking Chains

With the great difficulties that come with the winter season, the myriad of summer distractions or the poor harvest of fall, sometimes it seems impossible to break our chains. At times we are in chains because of others' doing and at times because of our own, but either way, we can break free. Steven Furtick has a teaching based on Paul and Silas's story in Acts 16 when they were in jail.[91]

1. The worst is when you realise you were in isolation and there might have been people who tried reaching out, but you wanted to be on your own, which is the biggest error. The devil knows with others you can break free, and he doesn't want that. (This was certainly true in my case when I initially fell into depression – as I detailed earlier – and shut down on family and friends. At that time, I believed I found comfort on my own, but in fact, I fell deeper into my dark hole until I began interacting with others again to slowly climb back out of it.)

   Paul and Silas prayed and praised together as they sang hymns to God in the cell and broke chains.

2. Steven further elaborates on how our perspective can be our prison or a passport. There are chains that can break your praise but note – if you have command of your praise, you can break your chains. Praise is more than an activity; it is a perspective that must be practised. If your hands or legs are tied, then use what's loose. Use your voice that's not chained up to give praise, and he will break every chain!

   I found these steps definitely were a part of what helped break my depression chains, just as Tasha Cobbs Leonard sings in the song 'Break Every Chain':

   "There is power in the name of Jesus

   To break every chain."

   > ♫ **To listen to the song:**
   > https://www.youtube.com/watch?v=ucY6NwQTI3M

You stand empowered to break chains when you praise and work on your inner being despite how things might appear in the physical. By knowing to position yourself well and grabbing the hand of others who are reaching out to help you, you stand strong with a shot in this world.

Finding Your Purpose in the Dark

Your Dream Is Not Dead

Pastor Joel Osteen[92] told a story of a conversation he had about his grass to help put things into perspective.

Joel was in his backyard one day and his grass looked so dead, brown and worn out that he called a landscaper to check on why it had died.

The landscaper had a bit of a laugh and said, "Joel, it's not dead; it's just not in season. It's dormant right now, but in a few months, it will be green and lush as can be."

Joel was anxious about something that was only temporary and thought that's the way it was always going to be. When he realised it was normal, he stopped worrying about it. When he saw it brown the next time, he knew it would be just another few months before it was back to green. (I got to see this process with my own turf project as I had it laid from scratch, green and lush in preparation for the house sale. I saw the turf go through different seasons, and I would worry how it presented for inspections and looked into how to make it green. When I finally came across this story, it helped me accept and understand the brown season better too.)

Imagine if Joel had decided to have his grass removed when it looked like it had no life and he thought it was dead. I have literally felt like doing it with the one or two plants I have been gifted, but when a friend of mine tended to them, they came to life again in full bloom and with such beauty. It was like a miracle. Some of us, myself included, tend to throw away or give up on our dream because it looks dead, yet there is still a lot of life in it!

The truth that I became painfully aware of years down the track after throwing away a few 'dead' things or giving up on certain projects is that the difference between those who succeed and those who don't is simply resilience. It's a muscle of bounce-back ability, keep on keeping on no matter what.

I have started exercising it with most of the challenges I face now and still have a bit more polishing to do. One thing I know for sure now is to never give up, and it will all eventually fall into place.

My problems over the years have appeared big, and they might have been in the moment, yet looking back with everything else in perspective, they were small.

> "For our present troubles are small and won't last very long. Yet they produce for us a glory that vastly outweighs them and will last forever!" (2 Corinthians 4:17 NLT)

Through Trials in Faith and Believing

> "6 In all this you greatly rejoice, though now for a little while you may have had to suffer grief in all kinds of trials. 7 These have come so that the proven genuineness of your faith—of greater worth than gold, which perishes even though refined by fire—may result in praise, glory, and honour when Jesus Christ is revealed." (1 Peter 1 NIV)

With Jesus's teaching as my guide, what felt like a cold, rough winter season was in fact a resurrection and regeneration of the new me to bring to life all those dreams buried dead within me. From the spaghetti of trials or failures as an individual and part of a married couple to separation and divorce, there was something good out of every bad when I chose to stand in faith and believe.

In terms of selling the house, the biggest mistake seems to have been not accepting that initial offer so that the real estate agents could have worked on getting a contract to finalise and sell the house within the first three months it was on the market. From that first campaign over the next two years, each three-month house campaign was like the high-pressure, intense Australian university summer school where you have the 'pleasure' of optional torture by taking courses that you would normally take in a semester over the summer break in a little over half the time. But each campaign was packed with lifelong lessons I otherwise would not have learned with an overnight sale.

After the house sale, I did hold hope that it was finally springtime, but the resettling was not easy going with my dad's finger infection (which did thankfully heal – another thing to be grateful for), and there was still a pending court case in 2020 with added adjustments for my failure as a power of attorney in how I processed the finalised sale finances.

I wasn't found at fault regarding the power of attorney charges in court and this time around the judge also ordered that my ex pay my legal costs for pressing those further charges. A very small part of the fee was paid out of the legal fees owed, but I was done with pursuing that any further. Either way, the success was in seeing God's handiwork with yet another ruling in my favour that I had not even asked for.

In that same year, my ex had initially made an application due to my failure to sell the house and also sought changes to the parental responsibilities. Considering the initial responsibilities agreed in 2018 were not taken up by my ex, leaving me with the majority of childcare responsibilities, he sought a lower percentage of care. He then dropped the childcare adjustments with no further explanation and sought to address only the power of attorney failures. I chose not to pursue the childcare issue further, as I had done all I could in the past. It was up to him to advise what worked best for him.

In 2022, he opened up a Magistrates Court case to pursue this and find a way to engage, considering the protection order then in place. The judge assigned around three months for the applicant (my ex) to liaise with the family relationship centre and his lawyer regarding what he was after and then advise the court. In that time frame, I didn't receive further information regarding what best suited him in terms of parental care. I turned up to court to hear what was finalised, but he was absent with no further correspondence to the court either, and that was that. I continued to work with what I had to keep standing and carry on with the sole parental responsibilities as I had learned to do in the past.

All in all, I got through each challenge I faced. In hindsight, it was preparation for future season cycles as I have improved how I handle difficulties that come my way.

You can make it through any season, too.

Just like Ruby Bridges, Kobe Bryant or Chang in *Chang Can Dunk* – aim to be the best version of yourself. One of Kobe's famous quotes is, "I don't want to be the next Michael Jordan; I only want to be Kobe Bryant", and he left a legacy that still lives on from his grave.

Be encouraged to go ahead and just be you by taking action today on that which is buried deep inside you. One of my favourite quotes that encourages us to act is from Collective Hub,

> "Fall in love with your future because it's yours to create."

Make a vision board, manifest, meditate on your heart's desire. It's there for the taking if you're brave enough to demand it.

The story of the song 'Am I Wrong' by singer-songwriters Nico and Vinz exemplifies this.[93] It is an inspirational, catchy song by two Norwegian artists of African descent. The hit song topped the charts in several countries internationally. They had millions of views on several music platforms and broke a record on Shazam as the most Shazamed song in the world. All this came from them partnering on their common experiences and vision, then sharing this by singing about their identities, their journey, where they came from and what they call 'an anthem for doing what you love', despite others thinking they had no chance of achieving those big dreams. They did it because they kept believing in a better version of themselves, their unique story and dream. It turned out they were not wrong. As per their song, the ABC News interviewer was cheeky enough to say, if that's wrong, then none of us want to be right.[94]

> ♫ **To listen to the song:**
> https://www.youtube.com/watch?v=bg1sT4ILG0w

I loved hearing speaker and author Lysa Terkeurst's take on David's story of finding purpose from his dark season.[95]

> "My heart, O God, is steadfast, my heart is steadfast; I will sing and make music." (Psalms 57:7 NIV)

David was in a cave that surely felt like a death sentence, an end to all he had hoped and dreamed. He lifted his eyes to God and by doing that, his heart was able to be shifted. At this stage, David had already been anointed to eventually become king. He served King Saul faithfully before he became jealous and was out to kill David. This made it seem very unlikely that David would end up sitting on the throne as the anointed king he had been told he would be one day. David went through hell on earth with Saul and now found himself hiding in a cave. This winter season birthed in him a heart ready to lead. It made him strong and created something new in him. He became a leader of 400 men who were in distress, discontented or in debt (Samuel 22:1-2).

As Lysa Terkeurst points out – darkness was the perfect training ground for David's destiny. Those difficult places we so desperately want to be done with can become good training ground for us as well. But we have some choices to make. Will we see this dark time as a womb or a tomb? Is it a birth, the growth of something new or the death of what we thought should be? Will we fix our eyes on the truth of God's goodness, or will we give in to hopelessness and despair?

> "Bless the LORD, O my soul, and all that is within me, bless his holy name! Bless the LORD, O my soul, and forget not all his benefits." (Psalms 103:1-2 ESV)

My dad shared the story of King Hezekiah with me. When King Hezekiah of Judah was being attacked by the King of Assyria, a great warrior who had conquered many nations, he was sent a letter by his enemy, which he took to the temple before God. The Lord defended and saved King Hezekiah's city. (2 Kings 19:14-36). When I was served with a letter for my failures as power of attorney (discussed above), I was blessed to have my dad around. He suggested I have a place of praise and worship in the house where I could bring my challenges to God or simply praise him to make my load lighter. (Others choose to go to a temple or church like King Hezekiah did.) I, too, presented my letter to God like King Hezekiah and as I waited on the result of the case, I was at peace. Jesus says when you have burdens, bring them to me, I will carry them, and I will give you rest. (Matthew 11:28-30). He doesn't say you need to carry them – that will only make you feel like you are being crushed.

In my different seasons when I seemed to have good matched up with bad, ultimately, good won. With a few falls here and there, I have learned to walk again after all has been said and done. I can sing, "I'll fall but I'll grow. I am walking down this road of mine, this road that I call home" with Nico and Vinz. I believe part of the reason their song became an international hit is because of how relatable it is. We all think we could be something for real, try to reach the things that we can't see and start to wonder if we are wrong to try when we fall.

There is comfort in their words as they sing that, despite it all, we should fight, keep going for our goal and not worry because we are not alone. What's inspirational is that their vision actually became a reality, so when we sing along with them, it's like doing it with someone who gets it in a real way. Having gone through different trials we eventually get to speak to those who are going through similar trials and let them know we understand. We can comfort them with the comfort we received.

> "3 Praise... God of all comfort, 4 who comforts us in all our troubles, so that we comfort those in any trouble with the comfort we ourselves receive from God." (2 Corinthians 1:3-4 NIV).

We change the way we dress according to the seasons, and similarly, we need to adapt accordingly to each season in our life, otherwise survival will be more difficult.

Joyce Meyer[96] shared on Psalm 23 – The Lord is my shepherd and how he leads us: We are given insight into how willingness to change enables us to be led into the pasture of righteousness and growth. An interesting fact about sheep is that they will stay in the same pasture forever if the shepherd doesn't move them, wearing out the pasture and getting infected by parasites. They need to be moved regularly to be healthy, as we need to move through the different seasons in nature and our lives for growth and well-being.

The Lord said, "You have stayed long enough at this mountain." (Deuteronomy 1:6 NIV)

When you find yourself having the same issues, problems or perhaps being mad at the same person, then the place you are is not giving maximum benefit and you need to change to get to a place of growth.

Joyce shares how life seems to be a pattern of 'letting go and taking hold'. She let go of a full-time job and began Bible studies at home to pursue her own ministry. When she let go of her job, she thought God would bless her family financially and expected miracles. For six years, she had to believe in God for money to pay for socks, underwear and bills. She had done what she believed to be the right thing but saw it all move backwards before it began to move forward.

Sometimes our commitment is going to be tested. At that time, you are faced with the question, am I going to do things the right way or my way? Should I do what I want to do or what God wants me to do? Doing what is the right way or what God wants you to do always gives peace despite its challenges, even if people might not see it that way, prosecute, insult or make fun of you.

An album and single that resonates with me along the same lines is 'Godsend' by Riley Clemmons. It is from her season of change and growth and highlights how nothing in our lives is wasted.

> ♫ **To listen to the song:**
> https://www.youtube.com/watch?v=0GCgg1PMnqg

It's easy for us to remember the negatives – the hurt, pain, disappointment, failure. But we need to remember the positives – our dreams and what God promised. If we do this, keep believing and declaring, our long-buried dreams will come back to life, just like they did for Joseph, the dreamer who was sold into slavery by his jealous brothers to kill his dream. Through his resilience, he later rose to a position of power.

> "A river cuts through rock not because of its
> power but because of its persistence."
>
> *Jim Watkins (motivational speaker)*[97]

Just like all the stories of those who have made it despite the tough seasons, your stumbling block turns into a stepping stone, and you will rise higher. Even when the vision looks dead, be persistent, work towards your goals, your purpose and in due season, you will become everything that you were created to be.

CONCLUSION

You Are Chosen & Loved

> "12 My command is this: Love each other as I have loved you … 16 You did not choose me, but I chose you and appointed you so that you might go and bear fruit—fruit that will last—and so that whatever you ask in my name the Father will give you." (John 15:12-16 NIV)

With the understanding that we are each created with love for love, with our unique story and purpose on this Earth, we should go big like Jabez no matter the circumstances. He was an honourable man, a descendant of Judah, one of the twelve tribes of Israel. His birth was a difficult one that caused his mother much pain and she named him Jabez, meaning 'sorrow, pain'.

Now in my dark and lost times, as I mentioned at the start of the book, I went back to the beginning to question my identity. Fortunately for me, my name was a source of strength and hope to bring my attention to who God is and who I am in him. With a name like 'sorrow, pain', the vibe is different, but ultimately, no matter what name I had, I realised that my identity is first and foremost that I am a child of God.

Jabez understood this on a deeper level and made a bold, short and simple prayer:

> "'Oh, that you would bless me and enlarge my territory! Let your hand be with me, and keep me from harm so that I will be free from pain.' And God granted him his request." (1 Chronicles 4:9-10 NIV)

Despite his name, he understood who he was with God. He had a purpose on this Earth to create a legacy for generations no matter his start in this world or how he was labelled. He chose to acknowledge God's divine power to help him rise above it, to expand and be with him in all that he did. God answered his prayer.

Jabez used that 'suffering and pain' label that we all can relate to in life to seek to be more. We should stand encouraged to do the same, expand our territory even when it doesn't seem conducive. If you are lonely, depressed or battling whatever challenge, don't ask for God to just get you through it, but ask that you expand yourself from it.

> "Have a crown of beauty for ashes, joy for mourning, praise instead of despair … Instead of your shame, you will receive a double portion, and instead of disgrace you will rejoice in your inheritance. And so, you will inherit a double portion in your land, and everlasting joy will be yours." (Isaiah 61:7 NIV)

I got to experience the meaning of this in real life at an International Women's Day event held in Brisbane.

From the different sorrows, pain and challenges a variety of legacies have been built by ordinary people like you and me out of love for others due to their personal heartache, to make our world a better place. At that International Women's Day event, we stood together with men in support to acknowledge and celebrate that goodness.

There was a story from a keynote speaker, Hetty Johnston AM, who established Bravehearts foundation in 1997 after learning her daughter had been sexually assaulted. She used her pain and suffering to establish a legacy through a program that my young girl, fifteen years later, is using in school as part of the curriculum to educate, empower and protect young ones from sexual predators.

At the event, there were many other stories, including a more recent one from another lady, Helen, whom I sat with at the same table. She is the founder of Share the Kindness and a cancer survivor. She struggled with breaking the news of what mummy was going through to her two young

CONCLUSION

girls. She thought of using beautiful ragdolls with removable hair as a way for them to relate. She found a silver lining in it, and now, some years later, she has a charity that makes the same dolls for children and families affected by cancer. Through her suffering, she wanted to leave a legacy that helps bring a little joy in others' lives during a tough time by providing a tool to help them process hair loss during their cancer treatment.

There was Haatsari, a best friend I have known since I was eighteen in my first year in Australia. We founded JDE foundation together in honour of our mothers' hearts and the teachings they imparted to us as children and as a memorial to my late mother and my friend's father. JDE aims to help better the lives of children in poverty through education. It also works with existing organisations to support and empower women suffering from abusive relationships or domestic violence through care packages that cater for their well-being.

As I sat down amongst these profound women, my story was still a work in progress, not as established as theirs, and to an extent, I felt as if I had on hand my two lines to a song plus a guitar with two broken strings like John Rzeznik working on 'Iris'. I had real-life examples before me that showed it could be done, from the grand to the simplest things. There was proof of a huge impact on the world from those actions taken. I had to work on my part as I continued to learn and grow in the realisation of my calling and purpose in life by taking one step at a time. I hope the same for you.

The year I founded the charity and began my writing, I grieved my mother and marriage. I then looked at what was left from the loss and how to bear good fruit that lasts from it. The foundation and writing are my remembrance of the goodness of God in my life. It is my story, my song of thanks and praise to God and all those who have urged me on to be where I am now. I am certainly not where I want to be yet, but I am also worlds apart from where I used to be, and I am deeply grateful for that.

God answers our prayers, so choose to stop focusing on what you don't have and focus on what you do have. Be thankful for what you have even if it's as modest as five loaves and two fish. Bring that little that you have and, in his hands, he can use it to feed 5,000.

From Seed to Sequoia

> "Very truly I tell you, unless a kernel of wheat falls to the ground and dies, it remains only a single seed. But if it dies, it produces many seeds." (John 12:24 NIV)

This quote from the Bible showed me that in Jesus's perspective, death can produce life or multiply. I was in fact buried not for death but to blossom for life from seed to sequoia.

'Who Am I?' is something I wrote in my self-discovery journey as a mother to a girl-child whom my heart now also bled for after feeling worthless as a woman, a wife, so very lost in my marriage, as a new mother, and as a person. I eventually found my worth, and it opened me up to the truth.

Who Am I?

I am woman, I am black, and I am African
Some say three minority groups all rolled up into one
OR are they the makings of a giant sequoia, of royalty, of a queen?
I am a queen in my own right
Even if labelled a minority in society, in this world – this I know and
I am certain I am meant to inspire a majority
I am someone important – I have a vision
I know my worth; I know my calling; I know my purpose in life

I am Ruvimbo – 'hope, faith, trust, believe'
I am Kudzai – 'respect, honour, glorify, exalt and praise' the Lord
I am given the honour to be called 'mum', 'mama' by our perfect little girl, best gift from the Lord
I am a mother to our beautiful miracle, Tinotenda Arianah
Tinotenda – Tino 'we are' tenda 'grateful, thankful' – 'hopeful, faithful, trust, believe' (Shona)
A reiteration of Ruvimbo
As if to say never forget who you are as you walk this walk
With the one outstanding difference in giving 'thanks'
As if to say – gentle reminder, always be thankful,

CONCLUSION

especially to fight a good fight
Wear an attitude of gratitude to focus or refocus towards your vision
Arianah – very holy (Greek); the best, excellent; Ari –
the heart / lioness of God (Hebrew)
I am the mother of the best and excellent and so
I am to be the best and most excellent version of myself, first and foremost
For me to give the best and excellence to her or any others
I am the mother of a lioness arising
I am a lioness arising, a queen

I give thanks for today and the rest flows from here
I am not buried for death
I am buried to grow, regenerate
I have food on the table today
I have a roof over my head today
I made it through today
Choose to live in the moment, take a day at a time
That makes me see there is good; even in the bad, there is good

I am grateful I am alive today
I live to tell my story another day –
Focus, refocus on what's good
That makes me see the same thing in a different way
As they say –
Problem = Project
Obstacle = Opportunity
Challenge = Chance for improvement
So keep on wearing that attitude of gratitude to the end
The sum of it is God = Love and he calls to love
Share the love and love others as I love myself for that is the essence of it all

I am blessed to be a blessing
I am not a victim but
I am a believer, set to believe to achieve and above all
I am freed indeed
I am a child of God and
I am in my Father's house

My worth and my purpose came from my darkest path in life when it seemed to me that my being a woman, black and African from Zimbabwe – those very specific minority groups – were a part of what got me to where I was with my marital problems. I had to find meaning and hope in what drove me to a dark space, which ironically turned out to be my source of light.

So, Who Are You?

> **Birthplace:** Earth
> **Race:** Human
> **Politics:** Freedom
> **Religion:** Love
>
> *Stev Fair*[98]

We are all different but the same after all. It doesn't matter if you have one, all or even none of the minority qualities that make me who I am. Whoever you are, you are someone important despite your circumstances or situation making you feel worth absolutely nothing. Remember the value of a new versus old $100 note is still the same value even though the other has been put through the wringer and is all dirty, tired and used up. You have your own unique story to tell, and you are someone of value.

Despite our different backgrounds, we all have these moments shared that the world demands to hear, your legacy for generations. Don't let those moments be buried six feet under because of procrastination, fear, doubt, criticism, depression, anxiety or whatever other reason. Use all of that to propel you and start with whatever you have at hand.

Motivational speaker Lisa Nichols says the key to having people listen to you is to share your story because you will tap into something within them from something within you. Through her words, her story, I found inspiration in – you. She says,[99]

CONCLUSION

You

"You are the designer of your destiny.
You are the author.
You write the story."

From this I see that:
You have the pen in your hand.
You can choose the outcome.
You tell your story.
You and your story are a blessing.

At a Riley Clemmons show in Brisbane, she shared a story of a time when her mental health hit an all-time low, and she had panic attacks. At that time, the last thing she wanted to do was write songs or pray even though she recognised there is power in it, and she had been encouraged to do so, just like I was at my lowest. In her story she spoke a language I could understand from my personal walk. The advice that I had received seemed useless until I took steps to place myself in a position where I could get the message. What Riley spoke about seemed to relate to my exact situation at the time.

Riley also found her own way out of her winter season to spring.

> "1 Arise, shine, for your light has come and the glory of the Lord rises upon you. 2 See, darkness covers the earth and thick darkness is over the peoples, but the Lord rises upon you and his glory appears over you. 3 Nations will come to your light ..." (Isaiah 60:1-3 NIV).

Your story is your legacy for this generation and generations to come. Who better to tell that story than a person who has been through it? We might have the common ground of having grieved a loved one, gone through depression, divorce or whatever it is, but just like we have hands in common, each of us has our own unique fingerprint in this world. In that lies your uniqueness and you can share that difference with the world. It is a lifeline that someone else walking in similar shoes needs.

Where Am I Now, and Where Am I Going?

"Is it better to have had a good thing and lost it, or never have had it?"

Charles Dickens, Our Mutual Friend

I don't think I would be where I am today had I not experienced all I have. As I move forward, I have a better understanding that there is a time for everything, which helps me navigate how I go about the time of year or season I am in. I also know that in that season there are everlasting, lifelong lessons to be learned, applied and shared.

> "There is a time for everything,
> and a season for every activity under the heavens" (Ecclesiastes 3:1 NIV)

Through my pain I discovered my passion, my purpose in life. I learned that passion originates from Old French, from late Latin passio(n-) (chiefly a term in Christian theology), from Latin pati 'suffer'.[100]

There are many suffering synonyms that describe all, and I mean all, I felt at my lowest: pain, hardship, distress, misery, wretchedness, adversity, tribulation, agony, anguish, trauma, torment, torture, hurt, affliction, sadness, unhappiness, sorrow, grief, woe, angst, heartache, heartbreak, stress, informal hell, hell on earth. I also found out that with God's word as my guide there was delight, a joy in it that led me to that vision and purpose in life. There was definite hope and growth, like a tree with the expectancy of bearing fruit and harvest in the fall.

> "Blessed is the one … whose delight is in the law of the Lord, and who meditates on his law day and night. That person is like a tree planted by streams of water, which yields its fruit in season and whose leaf does not wither— whatever they do prospers." (Psalms 1:1-3 NIV)

As we saw earlier with John Rzeznik's birthing of the hit song 'Iris' – what might seem to be your dark season, a dead end, could be an indicator of a change in course.

CONCLUSION

The lead singer-songwriter says that he is terrible with song titles, so he does it last, and the inspiration for the title came when he was reading *LA Weekly* magazine. He saw that Iris DeMent was playing in town, and he just liked the name.

Before this discovery, I admit I didn't know Iris Dement or her songs. She is a singer-songwriter and a two-time global nominee at the time of writing.[101]

Her latest album has been described in the following ways:

"'Workin' on a World' is an album about DeMent's ongoing quest to find her place, about passing the wisdom of the generation that came before her to the one that follows." – The *New York Times*

"'Workin' on a World' is ultimately rooted in the same fundamental project DeMent has been engaged in from the very beginning of her career: drawing secular, spiritual strength from gospel music, telling mystical stories about community and perseverance and finding meaning amidst modern alienation in the meantime. It's just that now, more than ever before, DeMent is urging us to sing along with her." – *Rolling Stone*

"This is a very personal letter about the moment we all share, and it demands hearing." – *Wall Street Journal*

This book is my personal letter and story inspired by others to get me back up on my feet. I hope you find nuggets of hope in our similarities to propel you forward despite our differences. I chose faith in the Word, and we all have our different journeys and choices. Pick that which applies to where you are at and run with it. You will land where you are meant to. I chose to root my faith in Jesus, the author and finisher of our faith (Hebrews 12:2).

"Be sure you put your feet in the right place, then stand firm."

Abraham Lincoln

> "5 Each of you is to take up a stone on his shoulder, according to the number of the tribes of the Israelites, 6 to serve as a sign among you. In the future, when your children ask you, 'What do these stones mean?' 7 tell them that the flow of the Jordan was cut off before the ark of the covenant of the Lord …These stones are to be a memorial to the people of Israel forever" (Joshua 4 NIV)

When the Israelites stood firm with God, they did the impossible with the Father, who is the 'I'm possible'. They crossed the flooded Jordan river to their promised land and took a stone to mark that as their reminder or testimony of God's grace and work in their lives. The many other writers, singers and people telling their stories through testimonies, teachings, movies and books I have included here have their work as a memorial to share with this world. I stand to tell my story of how I, too, came out the other end despite the circumstances and am still a work in progress. This story is my stone, my way of marking the good in the bad and the message of hope from the mess. It is now your turn to tell your story, to sing your song.

I have a free Gratitude journal for you to start your memorial here. This is to help you grow your attitude of gratitude through thanks and praise each day. Count your blessings and name them one by one. Feel free to start by looking for three good things about your day today. This could be one in the morning, afternoon and then the evening or however this comes to you. Keep going each day until this becomes ingrained in you.

Also, take note of any of the other ten affirmations in my story that have appealed to you and cultivate them in whatever way you are creatively inclined. Create your own artwork – painting, pictures, words, recordings or whatever works. As the saying goes, now is as good a time as any. If you leave it for tomorrow or when you are ready, you may never do it.

> "And let us not grow weary of doing good, for in due season
> we will reap, if we do not give up." (Galatians 6:9 ESV)

ABOUT THE AUTHOR

R.K. Choga was born in Zimbabwe and immigrated to Australia when she was eighteen years old to complete her further studies. She started the charity JDE Foundation in 2018 to help empower victims of coercive control and children living in poverty through catering for their well-being and education. This is her first book. From what life teaches her to put in action, she aims to inspire others to find something that works for them. She lives in faith, hope and love with her daughter in Queensland, Australia.

Ten per cent of the author's royalties will be donated to charity: https://www.jdefoundation.org/

REVIEWS

I have put in so much work into the book publication. I really hope you've enjoyed it and have found a message of hope to apply in your life above all.

I am an independent author and it's really hard to get publicity for books. It's also expensive promoting and marketing a book, but the single most helpful thing is other readers' reviews.

It would be greatly appreciated if you could take a minute or two to leave your written review on Amazon or wherever you purchased the book for feedback.

Thank you from the bottom of my heart for your purchase and time.

- Amazon US: https://www.amazon.com/review/create-review?&asin=B0CZ4M2DPQ

- Amazon UK: https://www.amazon.co.uk/review/create-review?&asin=B0CZ4M2DPQ

- Amazon CA: https://www.amazon.ca/review/create-review?&asin=B0CZ4M2DPQ

- Amazon AU: https://www.amazon.com.au/review/create-review?&asin=B0CZ4M2DPQ

Website: www.ezyazabc.com

FREEBIES

To obtain your free printable or downloadable journal to fill in via your phone or online using Adobe Acrobat for your individual use only, please email us with either one of the codes in the subject line:

- The Message FREEBIE female version

- The Message FREEBIE male version

Email: ezyazabc@gmail.com

Happy journalling!

REFERENCES

1. https://www.fearfullyandwonderfullymadeobgyn.com/what-does-it-mean-to-be-fearfully-and-wonderfully-made

LISTEN

2. Meyer, Joyce, *The Confident Woman*, Hodder & Stoughton, 2006, p. 8.

3. Ibid.

BELIEVE & FAITH

4. https://www.youtube.com/@elevationchurch

5. Ibid.

6. Sam Collier, *From a Mess to a Miracle:* https://youtu.be/XrGmMYtYawA

HUMBLE

7. Messenger, Lisa, *Daily Mantras to Ignite Your Purpose*, Collective Hub, 2018.

8. Ibid.

9. Bible (YouVersion) App Devotional: https://www.bible.com/reading-plans

10. Ibid.

PEACE

11. Pastor Lia, *Heart of God Church*: https://www.youtube.com/watch?v=b-YkJGdqwk0

12. Dr Charles Stanley – In Touch – ACC – 182 Fox Channel.

13. In the YouTube version of 'King of My Heart' – Steffany Gretzinger & Jeremy Riddle/Bethel Music: https://www.youtube.com/watch?v=pomqj7acJc4

CONFIDENCE & PATIENCE

14. https://www.proverbs31.org/read/devotions/full-post/2020/08/10/hanging-on-when-it-feels-like-god-is-holding-out

15. https://www.abc.net.au/news/2022-06-30/qld-hannah-clarke-sue-lloyd-clarke-inquest-domestic-violence/101079774

16. Meyer, Joyce, *The Confident Woman*, Hodder & Stoughton, 2006, p. 41.

17. Song by Bethel Music, Jonathan David Helser and Melissa Helser (Writers: Jake Stevens, Johnathan David Helser, Melissa Helser, Molly Skaggs).

18. https://elevationchurch.org/sermons/been-here-before

19. Joshua 1:9; Deuteronomy 31:6.

COURAGE

20. This work is in the public domain and can be published without copyright infringement: https://www.public-domain-poetry.com/robert-lee-frost

21. Meyer, Joyce, *The Confident Woman*, Hodder & Stoughton, 2006.

22. Bevere, Lisa, *Lioness Arising*, Waterbrook Press, 2011.

REFERENCES

23 Bethel Music and Molly Skaggs.

24 https://www.josephprince.com/meditate-devo/fresh-grace-for-every-failing

25 The Belonging Co. Written by Andrew Holt, Hope Darst, Mia Fieldes.

26 In the *Washington Post*: https://www.washingtonpost.com/blogs/therootdc/post/psalm-461-god-is-our-refuge-and-strength/2011/09/12/gIQAFsa0MK_blog.html

27 www.joelosteen.com

28 Songwriters: Christopher Brown, Mack Brock, Steven Furtick, Matthew James Redman.

FORGIVE

29 https://podcasts.apple.com/us/podcast/travis-barton-life-and-business-coach-ep-5/id1232016117?i=1000388521721andmt=2

30 Chris and Cameron's story: https://youtu.be/WTi4tq6GuvU

31 Walsch, Neale Donald, *Conversations with God*, Hodder & Stoughton, 1997.

32 https://www.youtube.com/watch?v=ZZbG0U-Og84

33 https://youtu.be/enkTl55IyPk

34 https://proverbs31.org/read/listen/podcast/full-podcast/2018/07/09/six-practical-steps-to-forgive

LOVE

35   https://www.focusonthefamily.com/contributors/chris-and-cindy-beall/

36   https://www1.cbn.com/cbnnews/us/2022/february/it-really-has-everything-to-do-with-love-ruby-bridges-shares-the-key-to-overcoming-racism

37   *Queen Sugar*, Season 1, Episode 3 – 'Thy Will Be Done'.

38   https://www.abc.net.au/news/2016-04-07/the-little-brisbane-cafe-changing-sex-workers-lives/7306434

39   https://en.wikipedia.org/wiki/Brooke_Fraser

40   https://www.lightsource.com/ministry/life-today/sheila-walsh-grace-pearls-and-living-a-yes-lord-life-978059.html

41   https://www.youtube.com/watch?v=Y3uCKU5dvG8

THANKS AND PRAISE

42   Chris and Cameron's story: https://youBretu.be/WTi4tq6GuvU

43   https://podcasts.apple.com/us/podcast/travis-barton-life-and-business-coach-ep-5/id1232016117?i=1000388521721andmt=2

44   By Upper Room. Writers: Alyssa Smith, Elyssa Smith.

45   Behind the Song: SURROUNDED (Fight My Battles): https://www.youtube.com/watch?v=OBN6mrptAWk

46   https://www.youtube.com/watch?v=aWOkbEMpTLY

47   https://podcasts.apple.com/us/podcast/kings-of-kings/id173001861?i=1000355848105

REFERENCES

48 Songwriters: Sarah Reeves, Taylor Drevan Hill, Anton Goransson, Isabella Sjöstrand.

49 https://www.youtube.com/watch?v=zQIFJtBe2hA

50 https://www.youtube.com/@joycemeyer

51 Ibid.

52 Meyer, Joyce, *Seize the Day*, FaithWords, 2016.

53 IN TOUCH – ACC – 182 Fox channel.

54 https://www.josephprince.com/sermon-notes/where-is-god-in-the-midst-of-your-trouble

55 The Message (MSG) https://www.bible.com/bible/compare/EST.1.1-12

56 https://youtu.be/Za-yGR3sbNw

57 https://youtu.be/wJghcUSZyK4

58 Words and Music by Chris Davenport & Joel Houston; Hillsong Music Publishing.

59 Written by Steven Furtick, Ben Fielding, Jason Ingram, Chris Brown.

60 Written by Brian & Jenn Johnson.

61 https://www.oneplace.com/devotionals/encouragement-for-to-day-devotionals-for-women/in-the-middle-of-ditractions-encouragement-for-today-december-3-2018-11801811.html

62 https://www.takebackyourtemple.com/3-ways-to-lift-the-spirit-of-heaviness/

63. https://medium.com/the-ascent/how-to-starve-your-distractions-and-feed-your-focus-66109dd75583 Published in Ascent Publication by Founder & CEO of Lifehack https://www.lifehack.org/

64. Ibid.

65. https://stories.uq.edu.au/alumni/2022/alumni-awards-2022/

66. *Queen Sugar*, Season 2, episode 16.

67. https://www.accelawork.com/triumph-over-challenges/

68. https://www.accelawork.com/live-moment-success-failure/

69. https://www.newyorker.com/magazine/2019/10/28/the-real-nature-of-thomas-edisons-genius

70. https://greatergood.berkeley.edu/pdfs/GratitudePDFs/6Emmons-BlessingsBurdens.pdf

71. This work is in the public domain and can be published without permission: https://hymnary.org/text/when_upon_lifes_billows_you_are_tempest

72. https://life965.com/2023/01/loris-story/

73. https://youtu.be/bqblf5hDf2k

74. https://youtu.be/-yp73QuqY3c

75. Words and Music: Joel Houston, Benjamin Hastings.

76. By Sabastian Magacha.

77. By We Will Worship.

78. Composer, Writer: S'fiso Ncwane.

79. By Chris Davenport / Joel Houston.

REFERENCES

WINTER IS JUST A SEASON

80 Rohn, Jim, *The Seasons of Life*, Success Books, 2011.

81 https://www.arhantayoga.org/blog/the-four-seasons-of-life/

82 By Chris Davenport, Benjamin Hastings & Ben Tan.

83 https://hope1032.com.au/stories/culture/guests-and-artists/2017/hillsong-worship-bring-christmas-studio-seasons/

84 https://www.presidency.ucsb.edu/documents/address-the-capitol-building-sacramento-california

85 http://www.pbs.org/wnet/nature/yosemite-full-episode/15156/?button=fullepisode;http://mentalfloss.com/article/92177/10-towering-facts-about-giant-sequoias

86 https://www.oxfordlearnersdictionaries.com/definition/english/regenerate

87 https://biglifejournal.com

88 Pemberton, Steve, *A Chance in the World*, 2012, Thomas Nelson.

89 https://youtu.be/TuvOE7Y3YgY

90 Bevere, Lisa, Lioness Arising, Waterbrook Press, 2011.

91 https://www.youtube.com/watch?v=cDWeDo4tLzE

92 https://www.joelosteen.com/

93 https://www.rollingstone.com/music/music-news/nico-vinzs-am-i-wrong-the-inspirational-story-behind-the-hit-180163/

94 https://www.youtube.com/watch?v=sw9VhEaJ1eE

95. https://proverbs31.org/read/devotions/full-post/2018/11/29/finding-purpose-in-the-darkness

96. Fox TV sermon.

97. https://flatwaterkayakclub.com/explore/river-quotes

CONCLUSION

98. https://www.goodreads.com/quotes/7903454-birthplace-earth-race-human-politics-freedom-religion-love

99. https://www.facebook.com/LisaNicholsFanPage/posts/you-are-the-designer-of-your-destiny-you-are-the-author-you-write-the-story-the-/10158752691509306/

100. https://www.oxfordlearnersdictionaries.com/definition/english/passion

101. https://www.grammy.com/artists/iris-dement/8748

www.ingramcontent.com/pod-product-compliance
Lightning Source LLC
Chambersburg PA
CBHW050859160426
43194CB00011B/2220